From the Streets to A Savior

Kendra Carter

BK
ROYSTON
Publishing

BK Royston Publishing
P. O. Box 4321
Jeffersonville, IN 47131
502-802-5385
http://www.bkroystonpublishing.com

Cover Design: Gad of Elite Covers

ISBN-13: 978-1-951941-12-3

Printed in the United States of America

Dedication

I would like to dedicate this book to God first and foremost. He gave me the vision and inspiration to write this book. Of course, my mother and father, Cheryl Brown and Kenneth Carter. One of the greatest blessings God could have given me were my parents, who made a very important decision to have a genuine relationship with the Lord. Oooooooh! How it made such a vast impact throughout my life and groomed me into the woman that I am today. My grandmothers, both Roxanna Martin and Adeline Stewart contributed so much toward my integrity and morals, I hold them close to my heart. Not to mention, my grandfather Russell Martin, a stern man of God that would come pick me up after getting into trouble. My grandmother and grandfather would take me to Burger King every time and get a whopper and ice water. Then we'd proceed to the Goodwill as if I had never acted up. No words needed to be said, the love surpassed all of what they could have said. Unfortunately, all 3 have passed away, but I'm sure we'll meet again. My stepfather, Lafayette Brown was an inspiration to me as well. He too is resting in peace, a man of God that spoke minimum words, but expressed his love through volumes. Love you all, every one of you hold a special place in my heart. Finally, my 4 little, big babies that I love dearly. They are my heart and soul!!! Joshua was an added treasure, my little precious beautiful baby……

Acknowledgements

I would like to thank my Lord and Savior again! I cannot thank him enough! I give a great deal of respect to the Shepherd of my church home, Dr. Walter Malone Jr. at the Canaan Christian Church in Louisville, KY. Pastor Malone has sown into my life by teaching me the truth through the Word of God. Therefore, I'm able to go out with the appropriate tools and prepared to tell others about The Lord. And not to mention, the First Lady Sis. Malone. The most modest, God fearing woman I know. I love you all and appreciate your efforts and good deeds toward all

Special thanks to Julia Royston and BK Royston Publishing for their publishing services for this book.

Table of Contents

Introduction

This book doesn't discriminate color, age, ethnicity, gender, etc. God's hand is extended to all who want to be in relationship with Him. At times, we get so caught up with the things of the world that we forget about God. Everyone has a street you journey down throughout life. Your street may be different from my street. My street was material things, trying to uphold a status, which had me caught up in the things of the world. Going through the motions and just being concerned about me. But, when you actually get sick of being sick and tired, you'll change! You just better hope it's not too late!!! WARNING COMES BEFORE DESTRUCTION!!! I used to set back and boo hoo watching, "Iyanla Fix my Life." At the end of the show, I would be cheering and praying for the people who endured such hardships. Here it is my life was the one that needed to be fixed, yet I'm filling my starving soul with someone else's happiness. While I didn't even own my own. After a while or at least once, I would adhere to God and not my own calling. HE had to convict me. He spoke to me asking, "What made me think I was exempt from His blessings?" He reassured me I had all types of access to Him, which leads to happiness. HE let me know HE can recompense everything I lost and allow me to recover from hardships just as well. I had to get a move on with my life and strongly tap into the access I freely have with Jesus!

Chapter 1

What Sparkles Doesn't Always Shine

What it's like on a sunny day in the "ville!" Me and my people's get up excited! Hops out of bed like it's Christmas! Haven't said a prayer, no thanking GOD or nuthin! It was almost like Christmas, because we wanted to see what balla was gone trick today. Or whose nice car with the 20-inch rims we could jump in. Just to look fly in the "ville!"

So, we start off strolling down Chestnut, working our way to Broadway. I had on my Tommy Hilfiger dress that fit a little snug and my all white reebok classics with no socks! Hoping that the tip didn't come up because if it did, straight back to Foot Locker and getting a fresh new pair for free! My people had on her Tommy jeans with the Tommy collar shirt. Jeans fitting to a "T", we were wearing 'bout an 11/12, squeezing in a 9/10. Thick as a brick, that's what the guys liked! Light-skinned with the pretty brown eyes! Although we loved to tease about it, but was never the type to give it up! You had to really peel and work hard, and still then they had to wait some months at least. 'Cause the more we held off, the more we got!

So, as we're walking down Broadway, we see this white Benz with 20-inch rims and peanut butter leather seats! I mean that sucker was bad! It had a booming system, came through bangin' that Master P. "Make 'Em Say Uhh! You see! There were certain TOP NOTCH rules in place that was a must that we had to go by. One of them for sure was never to bop to any dude's music! You bet not shake a tail feather or nuthin! Can't let them dudes think we just the ordinary! We didn't want all the drama and baby mama drama that came with the nicer things in life! We saw all the other girls give up the punani, but we refused to be treated any kind of way! Because once you give it up, everything changes and you ain't no different from the next chick before long! We had to do something different from all the other chicks! So, I did!!! And that was getting "TOP NOTCH" tattooed on my right upper thigh! What better place to put it, so when I would wear shorts or a skirt you could see it! Because that's what I was, and you needed to know that! So, when people would see us, they would holla, "Toooooooooop Noooooooootch!" Got us hype every time! But they would never know it! The key is to keep humble and not be moved! Now that's what you call swag!

We not running up to any cars when the dudes got chicks in there, because we don't want our feelings hurt! We claim to be "Top Notches!" We sat back and laughed at these broads acting a fool over these 'no good' dudes! We figured soon they be locked up anyways, and you just move to the next baller!

This dude we met was decent, but that's not what's important. We just knew we hit the jackpot! He wanted my people's, but I knew something was in store for me. He had a friend that had just as much money. So, we exchanged numbers and end up hooking up with them later. We kicked it and ate at Ruth Chris steakhouse. We were in seventh heaven! We have never experienced this kind of baller mentality.

One night, the police ran in the building and busted everybody! It was on the news and of course the talk of the city! We messed with these big King Pins that was all of a sudden exploited on TV. It was like the hype for us, but at the same time our 'help' was gone. It got crucial for us knowing that they would be gone for a long time, and here it is we've been getting our nails, feet, and hair done every week. Now, we were going to be out of money, attention, satisfaction, and most of all, our reputation. You know other girls like to see you fall, especially when they know that you're depending on a dude. So, what do we do, shoot to the next baller!

We couldn't do too much because we had curfews. And not to mention, we were only 16 and 17 years old. We couldn't turn 18 fast enough! I woke up to my mother hollering about me messing with my guy. Well, the guys who got busted by the police were now on house arrest. So, my guy would send cabs to come pick me up. I was literally in walking distance when I would go over my cousin's house. It began to get way too much for my mama. She found out that my guy had been in this drug bust! She wasn't having it! So, eventually she had my little tail shipped right to my father's house! Matter of fact, my cousin's mother sent her to our Aunt in California as well.

On the Greyhound bus, there I went to Columbus, Ohio. This was insane to me! It was like being in a boot camp! I had to wake up at 9 in the morning! I asked my father, "Why do I have to wake up so early?" He replied saying, "Kendra, nobody should be sleeping past 9 o'clock!" He said I should have been up and ready to go to the library! That was way too much discipline and structure that I wasn't ready to adapt to. The only thing that gave me a little sanity was the fact that I was able to still talk to my boo.

So, I needed a plan to escape from this army-life setup! I figured since my niece's birthday was coming up in July, I could beg my mother to let me visit. Well, surprisingly she allowed me to come home. I originally had it all setup to arrive in Louisville that night, so I could go straight to my boo's house. Then, the next day I could link up with the family. We couldn't wait to see each other! We got off the phone at around 2 in the morning. I was so upset that for some odd reason my trip had to be moved to the next morning. So, I wasn't able to leave until 10:00 the next morning. I had already made that call for him to have a taxi ready as soon as I touched down!

I arrived that next morning. It was minutes before I pulled in, and I received a call saying he had got shot! My heart was crushed, and I didn't know how to feel! They said he had been killed around 3:00 that morning. I mean, just being 17 years old that was by far the worst chapter of my life. It felt as if there wouldn't be a comeback from this. As time went by, of course the heartfelt pain of the loss was diminishing. I figured if I got his name tattooed on me, then maybe I would feel his presence at all times. That's exactly what I did!

Time went on, and eventually back to the limelight! But, not in such a hurry! So, I thought, my mama had another plan for me! And wouldn't you believe it, I wasn't even aware of it! She takes me downtown to this unknown building. We go in the office and sat down with this lady. She explains to me about different options of obtaining my high school diploma and working on my career at the same time. Then, here comes options of various states I'm able to do this in. My mama done sat me up with going to Job Corp! Awwwww naw! She still trying to stop my flow! She let me be made aware there was no more pit stops. And this was my only option. When the lady mentioned Florida, I was like oh yea! But then it was filled , so that didn't work. Then came the option of Gasden, Alabama! I had never heard of this place before! Within weeks, I was sitting in this dorm with a bunch of people from all walks of life! This is crazy! Everybody broke up in here, how am I going to survive! I'm already on their lil' payphone calling up my dudes. My mom had strictly enforced that I am not to come home except holidays. I'm like yea right! Ain't no way I'm going to sit on this campus with all these walks of life and be bored! Needless to say, I was catching flights every weekend! My mom was in awe, wondering how in the world I was getting home all the time. It came to the point that she would beg my guy friends not to send for me. Eventually, that only lasted for about a couple of months. The people there told me if I was too good for that place to not even come back. Say no more! I showed up at my mommy's house once again! I said, "Mom, they kicked me out of Job Corp and said to never come back." Of course, I edged the words a tad. She was livid!!! So, back to the street life once again! I hooked back up with my friends to tell them I'm home for good!

So, now we can finally get back to the lime light! So, we run into the just coming up ballers. We figured if we come in the picture now, then they'll appreciate us sticking by their side. Then, when they do come up, we'll be set for life! Didn't want a job, and wasn't going to get one either! Why! It was too many thugs out here with plenty of money making it for us. It's dirty money anyways, so why not share it. Do something good out of it and give to the needy! Then, there were the guys we used for just rides and small bets. They were cool, but just didn't have the potential to be on the level we were looking for. In other words, they didn't make the cut! Some of these men had nice stable jobs, but were somewhat lame. Like, their life was boring! We need a little action and a tad bit of thug in them. And let's not forget the swag, oh that is a must!

So, here we had the 'Victory Park' dudes! Oh yea! Uuuuuuuh who didn't want one of them! It was the pure toughness in their walk and talk. But at the same time, they knew how to act like a gentleman. But, mess with them the wrong way, and you could have been snatched. I knew my boundaries. My friend always looked out if I needed something. They just had the swag you got turned on by. Not to mention when they came through beatin' and driving the Monte Carlo SS with the T-tops!

For some reason, we never did mess with those dudes that wore all that red. Must I say they look like they had a nice piece of change as well and was quite fly! One of my friend's did date one, but he was too hard. I guess that turned me away from them! Or either it was the day I was over my friend's apartment across from the Masonic Temple. We would hang right near the window to see all the cars ride by. But one day, this car came pass and he looked up at us while he waited for the light to change. I saw him with all red on and decided that I would yell down as I pointed at my big letters on my GUESS belt.

I holla, "Gun Up Every Slob Set!"

Maaaaaaan when I tell you that boy looked up to that window and screamed, "B****, I'll come back and shoot up this whole building!"

"Shhhhhhh! SAY NO MORE!!!!" And that's exactly what I did! I shut that window and called it in for the night! Even though it was early afternoon! I walked my lil' self-right into my friend's living room far away from any windows. I just prayed that man didn't pull back up shootin'.

I grew older, still doing the same thing, but just a little wiser. Renting cars all the time, hanging out in the malls and in and out of town. Going to the Velvet Rose and Club 537, same ole' game. I figured I needed to step my game up, it just wasn't enough. My peoples went on her way, and I went on doing me. I began to have my Sunday routine. Go to church, cruise through and post up at Shawnee Park, ride dem rails at 'The Roost' skating rink and then hit up the 'Velvet Rose!' I was pretty much going through the motions. Hangovers from the club and walking in church that same morning with the same clothes on, at times.

I went to the Velvet Rose this particular Sunday. I met this tall, chocolate guy who was from Gary, IN. I loved his accent. He was real laid back. Just enough thug in him, but still the sophisticated mentality. He and his brother owned a clothing store and seemed to have his stuff together. We began to kick it. He took me to Jamaica and on big shopping trips. I mean, I was deeply in love with this guy! This time around, it wasn't about the money. He was like what I called an 'all in one man.' Until the jealousy and controlling started. I would get accused of talking and or being flirtatious around other men. I would never even be in their presence, and he would threaten me if I even attempted to look! Thank GOD I didn't have to live with him, until the day my mother kicked me out the house. I was getting good and grown, and she had rules that I just couldn't agree with. I moved in with my boyfriend. Even though I moved out, it was like my mom was still in my business. She kicked me out the home, but yet threaten to send the police over to his house saying illegal stuff was going on! She suspected he was another drug dealer and wanted to cause me anguish! Not sure what point she was trying to make by far.

It's funny how when you live with someone you thought you loved so much, that you'd be slow about going home. It's like you know he will be there when you arrive. After church, I would hang around until the last person left. We fought almost every day, some days I didn't know whether I was going to live or not. If he said some words to really hurt me, I would come even harder! I knew what would get to him and that was his dear mama! I would say in a hard tone, mouth twisted and all!

"Ya bald-headed mammy," That took him over the top! He would say, "Do you know what girls get in Gary for saying stuff like that?" As if I cared though!

He said, "Pumpkin Heads!"

"Ah really! Okay!" He came after me even more, but I wouldn't let up! We going in to the end! I didn't know if I would get sent to the hospital in a coma, that's just how bad the fights were at times. I took plenty of hits to the head that I was not deserving of. Matter of fact, no one deserves to be hit! Even if my mouth was bad!

This one day just put the icing on the cake! We had an argument, and the next thing you know I ran, grabbed a knife and swung at him! He thought he was going to put his hands on me again, I just wasn't having it this go around! I grabbed a knife to scare him off from hitting me!

He starts screaming, "B****, I'm 'gonna kill you!" I thought maybe I cut his finger when I swung the knife at him. He suddenly ran to the kitchen to put his finger under running water. So, I ran and locked myself in the room from him. It was frightening, I had to think of a way to get out with just my bra, panties and t-shirt on. I didn't have time to slip on anything, my life was in jeopardy from the sounds of him! I looked under the bed, and there I saw an AK rifle. As scared as I was of guns, I wasn't sure how this would turn out.

I unlocked the door and made a run toward the front door! With the gun held up high so it wouldn't shoot me! I looked at him and told him to step back! He looked at me with a closed mouth and didn't say a word. I was like G.I. Jane in an action movie, except this was for real. I finally made it out the door safe and jumped off the curve to my car.

Once I was in the car, I still had to worry who saw me and if they would call the police on me or not! I mean, come on! Me! African-American girl running with just a t-shirt, bra and panties on with a rifle in her hand! In the Old Louisville neighborhood at that! Once I drove off, I didn't look back!

Some time had passed and I must admit there was some loneliness. We talked a few times about reconciling. But I knew deep down that if I went back, I wouldn't come out alive. I went through a period of thoughts of suicide, depression, and most of all a lot of anxiety. I asked GOD to please make the situation right, so we could have a decent relationship. I just couldn't get him off my mind, even though it was a dangerous situation. There was no one else who could fill his shoes, at least, when we were on good terms. It just felt like I needed some real deal closure or something. All I know is there was this void in my heart that just couldn't be filled. When I woke up he was on my mind, and before I dozed off he was on my mind.

I went to Walmart one afternoon, and in the aisle was this baldheaded light-skinned thin built guy with golds in his mouth. He kept staring, so I stared back. In the midst of my heart brokenness, nobody ever said it was a crime to look! He began to flirt, and I actually took his number. If I felt like calling, indeed that's what I would do. As we talked for the first time on the phone, he mentioned he had been in the army. I thought okay, we may be getting somewhere. He said that he was in school to be an L.P.N. Same as I was, so I thought okaaaaay 'potential!' We could possibly help each other, because I'm on that same path earning my nursing degree. Not to mention, this would be my 2nd attempt trying to complete my nursing degree. Of course, it was time for a change, and it was exciting to me that we had so many things in common.

We kicked it every now and then. At least, as long as I felt like being bothered. He was a little worrisome at times with the calling. Of course, I liked that to a certain extent, but not all the time. We kicked it a couple of times, and one morning his baby mama came beating at the door!

He goes to open it, and of course first thing she says is, "Where's that "B" at?"

I raised up out that bed, even though I wasn't looking quite like a dime plus nine! But who cared, when I got finished with her, I wasn't 'gonna be looking any better! Now, I was going to start off being calm, but the moment another "B" word came out her mouth, it was on! She had a baseball bat in her hand and threatening to call the police for what, I don't know.

She starts cussing saying, "You got this "B" in here, and you were supposed to get your daughter."

You know first thing a girl will try and say something about their child, especially, when they see another woman.

But, I'm literally thinking in my head, 'You can have this lame, lying a** necka!'

That was way too much for me, especially me finding out everything was a lie! Here it is, I'm just trying to fill this void in my heart. I have to deal with all of this too! He wasn't in school, no army experience, and the closest thing he came to nursing was a street pharmacist! I left there to never return again!

Well! Well! I call myself spending the night just those couple of times and trying to get my ex off my mind. Even though I set my requirements straight from the beginning! I specifically stated we were friends and will remain friends, because I'm still in love with my ex. I'm sure he thought he would just become this man I fell in love with! WRONG!! Not by a hair of my chinny chin chin! All I wanted to do was just look like a doll in my red lace cheeky panties, with matching bra from Victoria Secret, prance around his house and then watch him drool at the mouth. While I was doing all of that, I go to the doctor and this fool done knocked me up!!! I told the doctor that she might wanna run that test again, because I'm sure I fall in that 99% bracket! Or it just might have been a false-negative-negative-negative, if that makes any sense! I just couldn't believe this nonsense! So, talking to myself, 'You mean to tell me that morning when I got out the shower, walked into the room, and locked the door behind me. I didn't need to see him, and he didn't need to see me! It just wasn't that type of party! He wanted to play games and roughhouse me.'

Then hollers, "Don't make me come in there and take that towel off you!"

I distinctly said, "Little boy quit playing with me!" Oh! That was his Q. Then he came in there so fast and somehow unlocked the door! Broke in the door and started to light weight wrestle with me, but yet he knew what he was doing! I'm trying to push him off of me, and he's steadily trying to get my goods! Next thing you know, he finally got up! Oh! Yea! I remember now! It docsn't take much is all I can say! I was pissed! I cussed, fussed and told him he took it without my permission! He laughed and actually thought it was funny! Well, I didn't by far think it was funny at all! The Doc said, "All you need is 1 sperm to fertilize a woman's egg, but there are millions that don't make it there!"

Me replying to the doctor, "So you saying a guy releases almost 100 million of them thangs, but I just so happen to hit the jackpot!"

"Why GOD?" I asked, "I don't even really like this guy. I mean it was supposed to be a friendly, cordial friendship."

I am now 2 ½ months pregnant and not happy at all. My mom wanted to attend the next appointment because she despised the fact that I considered an abortion. She was so against me doing that, so the doctor discussed me giving the baby up for adoption.

Immediately I said, "Heck naw! My child will never come looking for me later when I'm 50 or 60 talking 'bout, I'm your child!"

So that was out of the question! When we left there, my mom tried her best to convince me every way possible to go through with the pregnancy. So, I did. Once the 1st trimester was over, I felt so much better. My now child's father wanted to be at every appointment and around me 24/7.

I thought 'Oh no! I know it's your 1st son and all, but this is too much!' My mama was the only reason why I kept my baby! It was nuthin' for me to go and pay that little $400 to EMW. I would wake up to some ginger ale, crackers and not have that nausea feeling. I take the cramps that came afterwards any day.

Prior to my pregnancy, I had already had one abortion. This is why being pregnant was not up my alley. Especially, since it wasn't really my fault anyways. Besides, it's not even a baby yet. It's just a blood clot and hasn't even formed into a baby. At least that's what my big play sister said. She is the one who turned me on to the abortion clinic. She would faithfully go like making grocery runs. Her dude would drop that money like it wasn't nuthin'! My last boyfriend and I had to drop her off there at the clinic!

So, since my now baby daddy wanted to hang around, I said well, I could use some company. The baby started to grow on me. My ex is still on my mind. I even thought that it could have been his baby. I wished, just hopeful thinking! I mean, couldn't it be a coincidence because the fact that it happened so quickly with this newbie. I started back trying to find my ex. I mean just in case it was his. I needed to get him prepared. Apparently, he got word about me being knocked up by some Newburg guy. So, when I tried to call him, he would hang up. Oh, that killed me emotionally! Now I'm back to thinking how I'm carrying a baby by a guy I don't even care for. I still couldn't handle that, so I call myself going to the clothing store he owned. As I was riding on a back road to get there, I needed to be cute. So, I'm looking in the mirror and fixing my hair. I look up and

'BOOM!' I must have drove pass the stop sign right into this car! I hadn't paid my insurance and my car was totaled. I got summoned to court to pay for damages on the other person's car. I had to pay restitution that sat me right on down for a while. Needless to say, I never made it to the ex!

Chapter 2

My Help is Cut Short

So, my birthday had passed, but I would have loved to spent it with my ex as planned. Before the breakup, he had planned to take me out the country to Mexico for my birthday. So, I figured I needed to hear his voice and some closure. You know, just so he could at least wish me a belated birthday. I did just that! Oh my! When I heard his voice, the feeling was indescribable.

I said really nicely, "Do you have something to tell me?" He immediately said, "Ah yeah, Happy Birthday!" I literally begged him to come pick me up from over my granny's house. I told him I wouldn't call him anymore if we could just talk. After convincing him for a whole half hour, he considered. I was so anxious and ready for this moment! I had on my black fitted guess dress and was 4 months pregnant. But you would have never known!

I wanted him to think that I wasn't either, even though he had heard it. I didn't want anything to throw us off or make him upset. He pulls up in this rental, I jumped in the car and hugged him so tight! I didn't care where he took me, just as long as I was in his presence. We rode and ended up in Indiana driving through some side streets with houses.

Next thing I know he said, "Tell me you didn't have sex with him and got pregnant?" I stayed quiet because I sensed some heaviness in his voice. I'm lost for words and saying to myself where did this come from. So, he just kept repeating the same line over again. The more he repeated it, the faster he would drive through the stop signs nonstop.

I started screaming, "Please stop! You're going to kill us!" He did that for almost a whole minute, and I was scared to death! He finally slowed the car down and then exited on Arthur Street towards the hotel. No words were said, I was quiet as a mouse. We checked in, walked up to the room and laid right down. It still was nothing said, so I looked over at him to only see a tear come down his face.

I told him there still was a very small chance that it could be his baby. Maybe that would make him feel better, I mean it could. Maybe a 1% chance, but that's better than no chance. Next thing you know we just fell asleep holding each other. The next morning, he drove me back to Indiana to my mom's. There still wasn't much conversation after that. Everything just seemed calm and collect. I knew that once he dropped me off, I would never see him again. Maybe that was the closure I felt I needed.

I'm now 5 months pregnant, my family had the best baby shower for me! I was so happy, I felt more like a mommy! A couple of months went passed, I was laying in the bed one night and my ex called around two in the morning. He sounded a lil' tipsy.

He said, "If the baby is mine, I will take care of you and the baby. But if it's not, then "F" you." The phone hung up! I had no expression whatsoever. I remember immediately shootin' up a prayer request! Praying that the baby come out chocolate, baldheaded and a round face just like my ex! When my son came out, he was the exact opposite. He was light bright like his Daddy and looked identical to him! Oh well, I accepted it and back to reality. When I say he meant "F" you, he really did, I never saw nor heard from him since!

Life begins with a child. After my baby turned 3 months, we moved out into an apartment. I was working full-time at a nursing home and going to school part-time. Holding down a 3.0 grade point average and just had obtained my C.N.A. license. I had applied to Nursing school and was accepted, but dropped out again! When the going got rough, I would quit! I must say I still had that street mentality in me and was not sure if I was ready to let it go.

I still made my trips out of town to ATL. Lennox Mall was my thang, I would hang out all day and just shop! Oh!

Let's not forget about Neiman & Marcus store and my favorite restaurants on Peachtree St. If I didn't know how to get anywhere else in Atlanta, I knew how to get to that strip and that mall. All I know is I was in seventh heaven! I just wanted to ball hard and go back to the "ville" and stunt. I'm still in a rental since my car was in remission. This was my second wreck and no insurance again. Just bad luck comes my way with cars. That's why I make sure to purchase rental insurance every time. My car was too much to get fixed, so I just rented cars until I was able to get a lump sum to pay for it. I'm not sitting still to wait on nobody to come scoop me. I have places to go and things to do!

Eventually, I would get my car fixed, even though they called it a total loss. But to only purchase a burgundy Impala, you really couldn't tell me nuthin' with 2 cars! I maintained a job for a little while, but it just wasn't enough. Plus, I got tired of the same atmosphere. One of my OG's gets out of prison. He stayed only 2 out of 12 years and got released on probation. This is a true one right here, we kicked it every day. He wasted no time when he got out to get the things I needed for my apartment. Not to mention, he took care of all my needs. I didn't have to worry about nuthin.' My life was great! But, it wasn't long until I would get knocked up again. No way possible! Well, yea it was possible! This man just got out of prison, but this was not going down! And I already had a newborn baby at home too.

So, here I go to the EMW clinic and surely, he pays for it. He understood and respected my choice that I didn't want any more kids. It seems like when I get an abortion, that next year I get knocked right back up! Before the nurse rolled me into the surgery room, she had to get an IV started. She just couldn't seem to get it, so I told GOD if she tries again and misses then I will cancel the procedure. Well, the girl gets it, so I said I'm good to go! I'm still kicking it with my OG, and we just taking it day by day. He had a little side job, but he felt like it just wasn't enough to take care of all of his kids. He figured if he just made this one move, he would be straight. At least for a while, he had like 5 kids to take care of and said that pay just wasn't enough. He wanted me to fly out to another city with him, but I knew better than that. Something told me that wasn't a good idea. He made it back safely on his flight and that next day he was coming over after he took care of some business. I called him around 11 o' clock that morning thinking he would be done by then. He hadn't called me nor was he answering, so now I'm thinking he laid up or something. I called him for over an hour and even left voice messages! At this point, I'm saying

I don't care if he gets caught or not! Because he should have called by now, I am heated!

Finally, I get a call with his frantic voice! But soon as I pick up, I'm cussing him out asking him where he's at? He sounded like he could hardly breathe and said he was on his way. Here goes a knock at the door, I open it. He comes right in and walks straight back to the bedroom and falls straight down to the floor. He just rested his head on his hands, and I gently kneeled down next to him. I said, "What happened!" He raised up and explained the story. Once he picked up the package from this house, he drove off and noticed a truck parked. He had a feeling that something wasn't right, but he just thought about that money, and how he would profit from it. He continued to pull off, and the truck did as well. He kept looking in his rearview mirror to watch the truck. Once he drove through the red light and so did the truck, he said he knew it was all bad. At this point, he very well knew this was the narks. So, he sped up and so did the truck. Now it has turned into a high-speed chase! He finally escaped them, drove into an alley and threw the box in the dumpster. He had to get rid of the package because the police had a tracker on it, which would track him as well as the car. So, once he deposited the package and realized that there was no keeping up with his location, that's when he drove to my house. I was so shocked and felt so bad for him. I just kept apologizing for being ignorant of the fact that he went through all that, and yet I'm blowing up his phone!

I said to him, "You good now right?" He looked at me with this pitiful face and said, "I have to go turn myself in now!!" I said, "Whaaaaaat! Are you serious? Why? I mean, you dumped the package and never opened it up!" He stood up, gave me a kiss and squeezed me tightly! He said he would call as soon as they booked him. I was still in awe and confused at the same time. I thought, 'here goes my world crumbling once again.' He would spend the next almost twenty years in prison. One bad experience and guy after another. Now what do I do??? Life with a 3-month old baby, no income and rent due. Even though my child's father would look out and drop $200 every week! That money was gone before he even put it in my hands! Oh yes! My baby and I had to have the best! Fresh Jordan's and Tommy Hilfiger bibs and not to mention DKNY onesies! I did not play about my baby staying in the most up-to-date clothing and shoes. When I visited underground Atlanta, I would buy him COOGI sweaters even though he was still a little baby. I figured in a few months he would be ready.

So, I got a job as a C.N.A. that only paid $8.50 an hour. I wasn't sure how I was 'gonna make it, but figured I needed to step my game up. I enrolled at Jefferson Community College to take up nursing. But of course, I had to knock out some pre-requisites before getting accepted to the nursing program. I had always wanted to be a nurse, so maintaining a 3.0, car payment and rent made me feel so good. And of course, my help from the Almighty JESUS CHRIST. That lifestyle was nice for a bit, but that schooling didn't last for long. Again, it was in the way of me going to Club 537, Velvet Rose, and taking my road trips to ATL.

As we walked in Club 537 one night, there was this guy with such swag. He was peeping and so was I, but not too hard because that was totally out of the code. Well, he approached, and I bit just like a dog. May I say that the 'swag' got me in trouble and pregnant 3 times! The first time I got pregnant it was a shock, and there was no way I was having another baby. So, I had an abortion! I fooled around with him again, and there I was knocked up again. Since he was the one guy I was sexually involved with at the time, I just didn't want to hop around. Well, he ended up meeting a play cousin of mine at the club which was told through my other cousin. His swag got him in trouble this time. Of course, we were cool and somewhat kicking it. But to go and have what you call a 'one-night stand' with my cousin was off limits. My other cousin told them both that it wasn't right, but he told my cousin me and him were just cool. Off they went and eventually there I went! So here it is, she found out she was pregnant down the road. At first, I didn't believe it because he was denying that she was pregnant and said he used protection. He begged me to get back with him after apologizing several times. I wasn't hearing it at first! But like an idiot, I allowed him to kick it with me still. I still was uneasy with her saying she was pregnant and really didn't know the truth. We were lying in bed one night, and I had a dream that she was pregnant. It was really basic but so real. I jumped up like what was that about. I leaned over to him and told him about my dream, and he said, "Nah! Just go back to bed!" That didn't sit right with my spirit. Once I talked to her for myself, she admitted that the baby was his. At that point, it was a done deal. I definitely wasn't going out like that! Him knocking up me and my cousin! I didn't even bother to ask for the money to abort, because I knew he wouldn't want to. I took care of business and figured I would handle that later. In a hurry, I gathered my crew and headed for ATL! We found out it was much cheaper in Atlanta, and if you had a school ID, the cost was half. We picked up the rental, and was on our way.

Once the procedure was over, I went into the post-op room where I ate Ritz crackers and drank ginger ale. It was the best meal ever considering no food past midnight. When I got done, I walked to the waiting room and busted out the door saying, "Toooooooop Nooooooootch!"

"Let's go to the Mall, I'm ready to shop. They all looked in awe wondering how I got done that fast. Truth be told, it scared me a little too! I would have never been done that soon back home at EMW! We went to Lennox Mall and walked for hours. The cramps hit me once we got to the car. The cramps were so bad, they put me to sleep the whole ride back home. Back to the boring "Ville!" I thought I was done messing with ole dude, which was so lame to me after getting to know him. He tried to shack up, but I wasn't having that at all! I sent him right back to his mama's house! What the heck was I thinking about, and he didn't have no money either. Just a little ends here and there. But, since I didn't want a relationship with anyone, I just stayed content on an intimate level. That was sort of my go-to if I needed some. Welp, I tried to take precautions, and here I go again. This was my third time pregnant by this guy. I just knew it when I felt that nausea again. I'm thinking this is impossible, GOD must really want me to be fruitful as heck. I needed to make my way back to ole' faithful EMW clinic. I didn't want anyone to know though, and you had to have someone sign you in. The last time I let my son's Aunt drop me off, she wrecked my car on the side. My mom was working at the time and I begged her. She said, "Girl, I can't be taking you in this YMCA bus, I'll get fired! And you don't need to be doing that again anyways."

Well, I arrived to EMW clinic, I met a girl who was told she was having twins. They give you an ultrasound in the beginning to ensure how many months you are. Once they told her that, she said I'm keeping my babies. I'm thinking to myself, 'I thought we were in this together.' I was scared thinking how my body would react to another one so soon. They told me I was 4 months already. I was like oh no! After I get the money and schedule the appointment, it will be a 2-day procedure. I'm definitely not doing that because that is a whole baby. So, guess I'm keeping mines too. Like the first pregnancy, this one is growing on me as well. This pregnancy was quite different, I was actually having a second child. Something had to change!

This baby boy was born, and so we thought we would try to make it work. It was a total disaster and it didn't take me long to figure that out! He wanted to still hang out in the clubs and be too cool and too much of a player more than me! Shhhh! Like I told him, I wrote the player's book and published it! I'm too big of a cat to be fooled by a kitten. I just couldn't get over the fact that my cousin's child was born months prior to mine. Not to mention, he never acknowledged the child nor tried to have a relationship with him, whether it was a one nightstand or not! Even though he gave her the abortion money which was agreed upon by both of them, somehow it never happened. But regardless, she apparently made a decision to keep her baby which would be the best decision she could have ever made!

I applied for a job at the American Red Cross. I didn't know what I was going to do there with no experience. But, I noticed that they were hiring techs with experience in drawing blood which was preferred, but not required. I thought there is no way I want to draw blood. I will pass out! Well, low and behold, they called me in for an interview. It took a while before I received the call about being hired, but they hired me. I was ecstatic and finally felt like this was a new beginning in my life. I got that job and was able to land on my own two feet! We traveled to different counties and set up shop for donors to come donate their blood. It was so amazing to me that we could take a simple space, set up shop and turn it into a spot that would save lives. It was the greatest feeling ever! I met so many wonderful people and enjoyed my job. But I must say it was so hard to find someone dependable to pick up the baby. By him being almost a newborn, I couldn't just let anyone handle him. Baby daddy wouldn't help at all and couldn't accept the fact it was over. Asking him for money or to watch the baby was like tooth and nail. The times, when he did say he would give me some money or help out, it would always be something. It was always, "Wait or I give it to you later!" I would wait dang near the whole day and ask again. Then, it would be a big blowout and make an excuse not to even give it to me. That went on for way too long and was so stressful. I wanted to kill him seriously! That's just how bad it was, just horrible! But, thank GOD for his family that always help me a lot, along with my family. I can tell he hated me literally, but I remained unbothered. But at times, I must say I flipped!

The mobiles could hardly ever be dependable. Either we were late getting back and or getting started. Then, the money part of it was stressful. The baby's daycare needed to be paid and other necessities he needed. I thought very hard reverting back to dealing with my dudes. After dealing with baby daddy's inconsistency, never being on time, when I needed something for the baby was enough! At this point, I questioned GOD! I asked HIM, "Why are you making this so hard for me, and allowing this boy to put me through this?" GOD spoke to me and said, "Do you remember my commands? Or do you not know that wrongdoers will not inherit the kingdom of God? Do not be deceived: Neither the sexually immoral nor idolaters nor adulterers nor men who have sex with men." I Corinthians 6:9 (NIV)

"For ye are bought with a price: therefore, glorify God in your body, and in your spirit, which are God's." I Corinthians 6:20 (KJV) Oooooooh! Ding! Ding! No wonder I'm having all this trouble! Oh, how we forget the WORD! Especially when you're not reading it on a daily basis or not even reading it at all. I remember skimming over the Bible back in the day, but don't remember much about it. Yea! Yea! So okay GOD, I got to deal with it! My attitude did change a bit. I had to accept that I had committed this sin of fornication, repent, move on and do what I had to do for this child even if he never did anything else! It seemed like when I stopped the arguing and bickering with him, something changed.

Despite my role in committing this sin, I still had resources that were available to me. I didn't have to keep going through the financial part by myself. He needed to be held accountable as well. We both took part with bringing this child into this world. He hated the name, "Irv Maze," who was the Kentucky County Attorneys Association's

Child Support Committee. That is all I would hear. "Go on and run up to Irv Maze and get your lil' child support! B****, you only 'gonna get $50 a week." I think that might have been the last draw for me! My mom was aware of what was going on, and she hired an attorney which I was shocked, but thankful! She said she paid him $200 to handle the case and move it right along. I wanted baby daddy to be aware that I did have a lawyer named Darryl Owens, and that he was going to child support because of the lack of support! I called to let him know what was going on just so he wouldn't be surprised! I didn't have to do that! He said, "That old a** man ain't 'gonna do nuthin' for you!" I spoke not a mumbling word, and just nicely hung up after saying goodbye. Soon as I hung up, I thought, 'Wow, he is old!' That was nothing but the devil placing fear in my heart! I knew I had to stand strong and just trust HIM. But what baby daddy didn't know is when GOD is in it, can't a devil in h** block what GOD has for you!

So, here comes the court date. I must say it took some patience on my part. Who doesn't show up after all that big talk? Baby Daddy! They took me in a room and had me write down all my expenses. I was praying as I did it, because I wanted to be as honest as possible and just asking GOD to work it out as HE sees fit. I even put down my 10%

I put in church, because there was a line for that as well. I hadn't even really been talking to GOD at all. I would go to church, but still going through the motions. But, it's funny how when we need GOD, he's always there even when we're not thinking of HIM. My lawyer and I walked in the courtroom with all my paperwork and sat down. The judge asked was my son's father there, and someone said no. Within a couple of minutes, the judge said, "I grant you $165 a week, and I bet Mr. _____ will show up the next time! My mouth dropped so long and it was over just like that. I shook my lawyer's hand and thanked him as well as my mom. I also gave praise and glory to GOD! Oh, my goodness! I said to myself, "Man, this guy 'gonna kill me!" I just couldn't believe this judge granted me this much for 1 child, even though he was in daycare. Despite my sins I committed and all the heartache I went through, HE still showed me favor and how HE gave me double for my trouble!!!

The first verse concerning that matter that the Holy Spirit spoke to me was, "To which of the angels did God ever say, Sit at my right hand until I make your enemies a footstool for your feet!" Hebrews 1:13 (NIV). I can surely say this is true. Man!!! Things begin to start working out for my good! I noticed when I started getting closer to GOD, he started getting closer to me. Even when I would be in church, I noticed some of the things my Pastor preached about. I began to recognize and understand the WORD more. I hardly ever missed a day from church, now I'm not going through the motions. I have a yearning for getting to know HIM now. Sometimes I truly thank GOD because not everyone makes it that far. Some died along the way, BUT GOD's favor on me was amazing! Even though I wasn't acting like the Christian I should have been, I don't regret ever going to church when I was just going through the motions. I believe the WORD was still being manifested in my life like a seed planted and was just waiting to bloom. God was just patiently waiting on me to surrender my life over to Him. And oh, how glad I am that God doesn't give up on us like the World. That's why HE is GOD and GOD alone!

As time went by, again I kept having this feeling that the Holy Spirit had put on me. I've heard about the Holy Spirit, but didn't know exactly what it was. It just made sense. That was what I was feeling. So, when I looked it up, it said: "Flesh gives birth to flesh, but the Spirit[a] gives birth to spirit. 7 You should not be surprised at my saying, 'You[b] must be born again.' 8 The wind blows wherever it pleases. You hear its sound, but you cannot tell where it comes from or where it is going. So, it is with everyone born of the

Spirit." (John 3:6-8) And that's exactly what I was feeling and wouldn't allow me to feel any different. It was definitely a force that I felt and it wasn't going to stop until I acted upon what HE wanted me to do.

I had been wanting and needing to rededicate my life to Christ for a while now. I just kept missing that altar call purposely, because of fear and not wanting to walk down in front of everyone and all types of excuses. I guess GOD said, "You not getting out of this one!"

Chapter 3

Iiiiiii's Married Now

This particular Sunday, my Pastor Walter Malone, Jr. gave an altar call specifically for persons who wanted to rededicate their life to Christ. Oh my! Here is the altar call. I'm now feeling a tug in between humility (not wanting to cry) and scared to walk all the way down there by myself. Guess I felt a little alone, like someone should be walking me down. Then there was that feel of HIS force again, and I knew I couldn't prolong another day. Ok! I looked down my pew to only see 2 people beside me that I would have to walk pass. The WORD was so strong, and the Spirit was so heavy on my heart, that if I even opened up my mouth to say excuse me I was going in and just didn't want to do that. I was holding back what GOD was trying to release out of me. The Pastor is still making the altar call. Time was ticking! Guess I was sort of telling GOD the order and my limitations. Thing is, GOD doesn't have to do things according to my way, because it's by HIS will that we do things accordingly. Next thing you know, I took my hand to signal the parishioners beside me to excuse me. I kept my mouth shut like I said I was and then proceeded to the altar.

I started crying uncontrollably and felt a release and that heavy burden just lifted off of me.

Someone once told me when you get to new levels, there are new devils. That's for sure! I think people think when you get a closer relationship with GOD, that you're doing HIM a favor and that life will be flawless. Well not quite! By going through trials, tribulations, and hurdles is where you get your strength from. With that being said, life is going pretty good. In 2009, the good LORD allowed me to purchase a home. Obedience is the key for allowing GOD to just show up in your life and perform miracles! This was the most exciting time of my life, but getting there wasn't so easy! I had to continue going back to get my credit run every so often. We had to monitor my credit score as it gradually went up. There had to be discipline in the way I spent my money. I had to get approved for this credit card and put $300 on it. Once approved, I needed only to use it for groceries and or gas as long as I didn't spend over half of that amount. So, when it reported to the credit bureau, it would boost up my score and had to pay off some things on my credit report as well. In the midst of all that, there was a shift!

So, there was a fire in the apartment near me, and I could smell the smoke still after some weeks. They wanted to move me into another apartment, and that was not an option for me. The next time I moved, I wanted it to be into my new home. So that leads me to no other but my mom's house. I can save some money which is good. Oh, my goodness!!! There is 'gonna be hell to pay! I had a goal to be in my house by 30 years old. I wasn't 'gonna let anything deter me from meeting that goal. I moved in with my mom, and she immediately put the rules down. Curfew was set at 11:00 p.m. and here I'm 30 years old. Say whaaaaat! Are you serious!!! She played no games when it came to discipline. I was pretty much her wild child, and she was short of being slow. Oh well, I had to deal with it! One night, it was literally 11:07 p.m., and I just pulled into the driveway. I called in the house and asked to be let in, she said I was pass the curfew. She said my baby could come in but not me! Can we all say, "PETTY than a mug!!!" So, I drove to the Sheraton on the river and stayed. Let's just say that hotel became my second home. If I stayed there 10 nights, I could get a free room. Let's just say I received plenty of free rooms.

While out and about, I ran into one of my old flings. We went to high school together, and he always wanted to get with me. But, I was introduced to way bigger ballers in my time. We had always had an on and off thing, but he wasn't ready. He still had the streets in him, and wasn't ready to give them up back then. He called me and said he was getting out, and from that point on we would be good friends. He was a changed man I must admit, no more smoking marijuana or that street mentality. He was on the same page as me, just wanting to grow closer to GOD. We began to grow closer, so I figured I'd give him a try. I mean, he had already knew my kids from birth and they loved him! Everywhere we were, he wanted to be. So, I said why not. In the midst of me purchasing my home, he said he had a dream that once I moved in that I would quit messing with him. I thought, 'Oh my goodness!' It was almost like he started being a nuisance, see that was the old me coming out. He really was just loving on me really good, but I just wasn't ready for that.

So, I closed on my house Sept. 11th, 2009, one of the best years of my life! I actually accomplished one of my goals. I mean the good LORD showered me with blessings that were unimaginable. I received $8000 from the Obama program for being a first time home owner and single at the time. Then, I received $10,000 off the price of my home as long as I stayed in for at least 5 years. I mean blessing after blessing. When I sat down at that table and they handed me my deed to my home and my keys, words could never describe the feeling. All I could say is "WANT HE DO IT!!!" Goal accomplished by 30, so I ask GOD what's next? I think I did ask him a question but never waited on a response! So, I heard when you purchase a home, you usually buy a car as well. Huh! Don't believe the hype! I had finally paid off an $18,000 car that I cried about how high the monthly payment was. I was 'gonna ride it to the wheels fell off. Well, I had a couple of days where my car wouldn't start up on my way to work. It just did what it wanted to do. So, I told GOD, if this car makes it to Indiana where Kevin Willis is, then I'm definitely purchasing a new car. He introduced me to all these beautiful new Camry's, and I was in awe. Like, scared of a car payment, but did want something more dependable and having a mortgage on top of that was a lot! Mr. Green was having some chest pains and needed to go to the E.R. This man was still trying to conduct business inspite of. He has always been a hard-working and dedicated man. I felt a little pressured, because I knew he needed to get to the hospital, so I just said go ahead with the paperwork. We go inside to the only 'Mr. Green,' who already sold me my first car when I was 20 years old. I walked out of there in an all-black 2009 Camry SE with sunroof and all. Say whaaaaat! You already know what time it is! Going to get my car tinted and shined up by of course Kidwell's! I pulled out of there like new money! I was riding fly alright and at the same time had this $460 car payment, and not once did I add up my income for the month and what I could or couldn't afford.

Well, I got myself in this, so I had to deal with it! And mind you, I couldn't turn back to the streets or the men in them! There was no absolutely turning back! Still had my longtime friends and OG I would talk to every now and then. Round this time, my son had his birthday party at the skating rink, and I had all 3 of my friends there. Nobody knew who was who, but everybody blended in just like a family! My girlfriend said, "You just a player, aren't you?" I said, "Nah! Just all friends!" I hadn't made any commitments, so I didn't see a thing wrong with it! Although, they all wanted to commit, I wasn't ready. I mean, I do have this new home, new car, and doesn't a husband follow? Here I go again with the 'learned behavior' mentality. In other words, thinking as of the world and having worldly ways. I recalled praying for GOD to send me a husband that knew the streets and could understand what I've been through. Not quite sure why I asked that prayer the way I did, but I did……..

Eventually, I would start to express my feelings to him. I was still on clink clink and my body was on lockdown! It had been 3 months already, and he still was this great person that would do anything for me and the kids. Practicing celibacy was even more important to me at this point! I figured if he waited that long and was still treating me this good, then he's a keeper! So, as we grew closer the intimacy was at a high. He had been talking about getting married, but I pretty much blew it off. I didn't think now was the time.

Since this longtime friend of mine was stepping up to the plate, I began to like him more and more. He paid for most of the nights at the Sheraton hotel when my mom wouldn't let me in. You would have thought we were married, because we were together all the time literally! I hadn't reached the point to tell him I loved him yet though. Every time he would hang up the phone, he would tell me he loved me. He would finally ask me one night why I would never say it back. I kind of laughed it off, and told him that I didn't love him. It was way too soon to be saying all that, regardless how many years I knew him. You don't just jump on board and express strong words like that to someone. You have to think, he was just getting out of jail and still on probation. Even though you wouldn't know, because he carried himself so well. He was a very mannerable man, and I saw a huge change in him. He had always been cool though, just the streets and drugs had him acting different at times.

There I went, committing fornication. I even stopped him from spending the night to prevent the temptation. That just didn't work, he couldn't seem to keep his hands to himself. That weighed on my soul so heavy that I had to turn to the WORD. I was reading my Bible and came across 1 Corinthians 6:9 (KJV) and it read: "Know ye not that the unrighteous shall not inherit the kingdom of GOD? Be not deceived: neither fornicators, nor idolaters, nor effeminate, nor abusers of themselves with mankind….." I was convicted and remembered that as you get closer to GOD, you should be and think wiser. I should no longer be on breast milk but solids by now. I have been growing closer to GOD and know that this is completely wrong! I knew at this point I was hindering my WALK with JESUS! With that being said, we agreed to practice celibacy. We tried and would constantly slip up. So, there I ran across another verse in my Bible that read: 1 Corinthians 7:8-9 (NIV)"Now to the unmarried and the widows I say: "It is good for them to stay unmarried, as I do. But if they cannot control themselves, they should marry, for it is better to marry than to burn with passion." Welp, I definitely don't wanna go to hell over having sex before being married.

At the beginning of my work day, I started to feel some light cramping. I noticed some blood on my pants. I had to leave work suddenly and called my significant other to meet me at the hospital. We sat in the waiting room for way too long! I began to bleed even more, so much so that when I stood up, the seat was soaked with blood as well as my pants. I also had cramps that continued to worsen as well. He kept going up to the window asking how much longer we had to wait, and he expressed that I was bleeding severely! The lady expressed that they have patients in worse condition. Oh well, but all the while I'm walking back and forth to the bathroom trying to put paper towel in my panties to soak up the blood.

Finally, they called me back and laid me on a bed only to discover I was having a miscarriage. I was still bleeding profusely with no pain medication. The doctor explained to me he had to perform a D&C which is a dilation and curettage. It is a surgical procedure where they had to go in my cervix to remove any unwanted tissue. He then placed my legs in stirrups as if I was having a baby. I learned later it was almost identical as an abortion. Before, I had to sign paperwork to get an abortion at the clinic. But this time, it was beyond my control. My baby was being taken out of me, and there was nothing I could do about it. As he stuck his gloved hand up me to pull out the unwanted tissue, there was a biohazard bag right below me. This was so that everything he pulled out of me could be swept into the bag. I don't recall one bit of pain medication throughout the whole process until afterwards. Apparently, he couldn't get it all out and had to result to another option. He had to perform a procedure known as 'suction aspiration,' the doctor uses a hollow tube called a 'cannula.' That is then attached to a vacuum device which is passed through my vagina and into my uterus where it sucks everything through that tube, because there was still tissue in there. Again, it's the same procedure done when you get an abortion, but the difference is I am totally awake! My now significant other put on his gloves, and as I tried to push the rest of it out, he would sweep it out into the bag. The doctor just left me there in position and said to let the rest pass out of me. As my 'other' was helping to sweep the tissue out, an unfamiliar thing came out! That 'thing' was something that looked like a very tiny bluish- looking figurine which was my baby.

You could see what looked like was the eyes and all, that was so frightening to me! I began to be filled with a lot of mixed emotions. Of course, I thought back when my legs were up in stirrups having those abortions. I was thinking back then, just by heresy that the baby hadn't even formed yet. That was a lie from the pit of hell! It was by far more than a blood clot, but my baby just had not fully developed all the features. I mean it looked just like a very premature baby. That was very hardening to my spirit to know that I have aborted real life babies that I thought were not even formed. I mean it's bad either way, but I would never get another abortion just from this disheartening experience.

Another day's journey, I just slept that following day. I had to take off for 2 days after that to heal and just get my mental status back up to par. Weeks later, my now boyfriend looked at me, and said he wanted to try again for another baby. I looked at him like he was crazy and told him, "I don't think we were trying the first time!" It was out of disobedience! After all that, I felt like marrying him was just the right thing to do according to that verse I read. In my heart, I really didn't want to get married, but I didn't want GOD to come back and I'm sleeping with him and go to hell for fornicating or any other sin. Although, I did notice some things I didn't particularly care for like him walking away, not communicating and just shutting down over minor things. But, I figured it would pass, and we could work through it.

One day I called myself shutting the door to prevent him from walking out. I was the one to talk things over easily, but I couldn't just let him think he could continue not to resolve disputes. So, I shut the kid's door to their room, so they wouldn't think we were arguing. He told me again that he didn't wanna talk right now and to not confine him by shutting the door. I wasn't hearing that despite he had not been out of jail long and didn't like to be closed in. I slipped back quickly into the 'old self,' and told him yes we are going to talk, and I don't wanna wait! I mean, I needed answers and a solution to this small altercation that could've been handled right then. Finally, I stood in front of the door as he tried to grab the handle. He then picked me up, turned me to the side and sat me down on the air mattress we had at the time. I tried to get up and noticed my knee was turned the opposite direction. All I thought about was my kids knowing something was wrong and would be ready to go off on him! Mostly my older child that you couldn't let anything get by. I wasn't sure if my knee got dislocated when he picked me up suddenly or when he sat me down rather hard. I mean I'm trying to literally push my knee cap back into place regardless of the excruciating pain! I couldn't let my kids see me in this much pain!

He was in shock himself wondering too how it happened so quickly. He actually thought I was playing at first. My eldest son came flying out of that room and looked at me to ask me what was wrong. My son looked at my significant other with this mean face like he wanted to kill him! I immediately told my son that he didn't do it and that we were just playing and I fell. I told my significant other to call the ambulance, because I couldn't move and was in extreme pain! He was still standing there in shock. Once the ambulance arrived and put me up on that stretcher, I thought I was going to lose it! The pain was so great in my knee that it was almost unbearable to move me from one place to another. I just kept whispering JESUS. All I could say.........

Finally, we pulled up at the hospital. Thank GOD no more bumps and thumps against my knee. That ride was rough! Him and the kids followed behind the ambulance. I think all of us were still in disarray. The doctor asked me a couple of questions, like was I pregnant. He had to run a pregnancy test to know what medicines to use to sedate me I assumed. He came back and said I was pregnant! Next thing you know I was out. I'm not sure if it was because of the surprising news he just gave us or if he put me to sleep. Shhhh! That's enough information to knock anybody out! I woke up which seemed like just minutes and ask was it really over that quick. I had a black leg brace on my leg and the pain was gone just like that! He wouldn't leave my side. We stopped at Walgreens to pick up my medicine and drove home. He was very attentive and apologetic. I guess there was something to take from this incident. I learned not to enclose a man in, especially in a heated situation. I've learned my lesson! Here I am off for 3 whole weeks. You barely get that much time in a year for vacation! I was never the one to call in, but to be late that I was. So, that was all my vacation and sick time used up.   So now that we have this surprising news of me being 3 months pregnant, what now! Well, we had to accept it. That comes with the territory of having sex. At this point, I felt like we needed to make a decision quickly! No sense of keep fooling around and not commit to one another, because it doesn't look like neither of us is going anywhere, and I'm pregnant! So, why not tie the knot.

So, we pick up the marriage certificate. They had a list of people the courthouse gave us who were licensed to marry couples. We did just that. Scheduled a Pastor whom we didn't know to marry us. I was shocked that it was so easy and quick to do!   We needed 2 witnesses, that made me a little distraught. And the fact that I was really about to say, "I do!" I had already called my sister, and her response was that she had a headache. Not sure why I didn't call other family members, but I figured we'd notify them and have a reception later. I thought, this is a very special day for me and that's all my sister can say! I couldn't ask my mom to be a witness, because she just so happen to be in Florida. My significant other ran to his Granny's to get his black suit jacket to wear. When he came back, I was sitting on the bathroom counter crying. He looked and said, "What's wrong? Why aren't you ready?" I explained, "Maybe we should wait. I mean nobody is available on my side to come!" He told me that his mom and stepdad could come. I also told him how I was feeling, and he said, "Who cares what anybody says or thinks. I'm 'gonna be your husband, not them. I will always be there for you." And he told me not to worry about them, this is all us. That was true and it made me feel like I could depend on him solely, and he wouldn't let me down. Alongside with his mom and step-dad, I mean it felt like we were in front of 1000 people. The minister had on his black robe, suit, tie and all. This was real deal Holyfield! All of our kids were there. And even after marrying, my now father-n-law gave us $100 as our gift. I thought that was so sweet of him. Then, my now mother-in-law told us to pick a venue to hold the reception, and she would pay for it. That meant a lot to me. Everything just fell right into place.........

So, with that being said, we were united as one in marriage. Everything had been confirmed like when he was locked up. I wrote him once and visited him once. And that was within the 2 years he was gone. So, we were still friends, and he showed me this letter he wrote. Actually, he told me about it and didn't want to show it to me yet, because he wanted to see if it would manifest. But after a while, I demanded to see it! He drew it up like a map with symbols and organized what was important and prioritized it as well according to the different symbols. A couple of the goals was to have a relationship with GOD, to marry me and have kids. He said that's why he didn't even want to tell me about it. I was anxious though and wanted to know immediately. He never should have mentioned it. Oh well, that pretty much validated my decision that he had already had these goals in mind, and the fact I had already prayed to GOD about sending me someone who could relate to my background. I heard you have to be detailed when you ask for things, and that I did!

Iiiiiiiiiiiis married now!!!! I'm so elated!!! And now we can have sex all day long and feel good about not sinning! Though I had to tell him to calm it down, my GOD! I don't know how many times I had to tell him that! Like come on! We have a lifetime for all the sexual moments possible! We don't have to get it all in, in one day! Time goes on and here I am pregnant again! This makes the third time already, at least this baby is not born out of wedlock. Finally, I did something right! Guess GOD was restoring us another child in place of the baby we lost. I had 2 older kids already that were 7 & 11, and frankly, I didn't want any more children. But, that comes with the territory.

So, my now husband has been holding down these temporary jobs. It's time for a real job with real benefits, because this baby was surely coming. When he first got out, he couldn't really find a job, so he started out at a landscaping job. Even though it didn't pay a lot, I was just happy at the fact he humbled himself to work somewhere he had no interest in. Then, he also sold phonebooks out of the car. Before he even got paid, he was already asking me what needed to be paid. That didn't surprise me because he was doing that even when he wasn't living there. I did admire him for taking the initiative to step up.

One thing I did notice, is that he would see those checks and get frustrated about the check being so small. I would remind him constantly that GOD will provide and that sometimes you have to take baby steps before GOD allows you to run! I would often tell him and reassure him that I was so proud of him not going back to the streets and smoking marijuana. Which he couldn't anyways, because he was still on probation. Well he could, but he would be in violation. He responded saying, "You couldn't pay me to go back to doing any of those things ever again!" Well, that's one thing I didn't have to worry about! We continued to pray for a better job, pay, and permanent job.

Chapter 4

Kill It Before It Kills You

One Sunday afternoon after coming home from church, my mother stops by with a friend from church. Actually, she had just met this lady in her Sunday School class. My mom introduced her to me and my husband, and explained that she was a supervisor at Tyson Foods. May I say, by the time she left, she had given my husband every piece of information he needed to apply for the job. She even told him to call her as soon as he submitted the application. He was hired within 2 weeks, look at My GOD! We had benefits and stability now. Life was going pretty smooth, although it was far from perfect! Anytime there was a disagreement of any sort, he tried to ignore the situation. Never ever would anything get accomplished, nor would we re-visit the problem to find a solution.

Well, this started to be a habit for him. After a year of him working at Tyson, I noticed significant changes like more short tempers, holding grudges, and just shutting all the way down. He would even have a couple of altercations with some employees, but I would always remind him how the devil doesn't like that he's been holding down a job and going to church consistently. I knew something was going on with him, but didn't know what. He finally landed this great job, and I just couldn't fathom what was wrong now! He also began to leave out and say he was going for a ride to cool off. When he would come back, he'd be so content. But still in all, the situation never was handled. It got to the point that it would occur almost every 3 months or so! A couple of times at that! And on top of that, I was pregnant again! So, here I am with all these kids and carrying another child. Seven months later, my husband would walk out at least 2 more times staying gone for a day and sometimes 2 days coming back on either Saturday sometimes or Sunday, depending on what he felt. I got to the point where I didn't even want to call him when he left, not even to ask for help with the kids. I just kept calling on JESUS, but at the same time asking him what is going on. I mean I have heard marriage is great that first year, and thereafter it can be rough for the next 5 to 10 years. Oh my! I don't think I have it in me. It's already been a couple years, and I'm experiencing this! I know for sure I didn't sign up for this! Well, this too shall pass hopefully……

So, it is July 10th and the kids and I had been to church and heard an inspiring sermon. We pull up to notice an unfamiliar car in the driveway. This big red F-150 truck, and who gets out, hmmmm the hubby. Oh, how could I forget, he got in a car wreck and he had to get a rental while his car was getting fixed. He was in some pain, so the chiropractor prescribed him Lortabs. Well of course, if you complain of pain, they sometimes prescribe you Lortabs known in the streets as 'tabs.' It's used to treat pain but can also be a high risk for addiction and dependence, meaning you could get addicted to this pill. Of course, he comes back on a Sunday evening where he knows my heart is a tad bit softer, because I've been to church so he thought I guess. That got taken advantage of way too many times. He offers to take us out to eat, except he wanted to drop the kids off thereafter so we could talk. So, I'm like okay! After eating and dropping the kids off, he wanted to walk down on the waterfront. It was such a gorgeous day, and we just walked and talked. He would say how sorry he was for everything, and ask if I could please give him another chance to make it right. Of course, I did again! Now remind you, I am just a couple of days from going in for a scheduled C-Section. So why wouldn't I take him back. I needed him at this point. He's going to be there anyhow, because he has to help me with the kids and our new baby.

So, we pick up the kids on that beautiful Sunday afternoon and go home. Yes, of course we went through the normal routine. After getting the kids ready for bed, we pray, read the kids the veggie tale devotional, tuck them in real tight and we make love as if it was our first time. I would always re-iterate my standards and that I was not going to tolerate any more walking out just because something didn't go his way, or he didn't want to communicate. He would agree with tears rolling down his face like he was the happiest man and was 'gonna do right this time! After getting out the shower, I noticed he had already laid down. At first, I didn't want to wake him. But I started to feel some sharp pains and just thought it would bypass, so I proceeded to get in the bed. The pain got way worse. I awoke my husband to tell him I was having some sudden sharp pains in my stomach. We immediately got in the car and flew to the hospital, which was about 20 minutes away, but it seemed like forever. What I figured was contractions were starting to forcefully get closer and closer. I mean they were getting unbearable at this point! I have never experienced labor with my previous kids. After the umbilical cord was wrapped around my first child's neck, the doctor had to perform an emergency C-Section. Thereafter, he recommended me to always get a C-Section if I were to have any more kids. So, this was new to me because I never went through labor. I advised my husband to call 911 on the way there to let them know we were driving extremely fast on the highway towards Baptist East Hospital. The last thing I wanted was an altercation with the police to stop us! At the same time, he was trying to call the emergency line to get in touch with my doctor.

Finally, we pulled up in the emergency zone. Right before I got out the car, I felt a thump and another thump, like an up and down motion and then what felt like a bust right near my vagina. They came with a wheelchair as soon as I got out the truck asking me questions I couldn't even answer. I was still in shock and really didn't know what was happening with my baby. The nurse lifted me on the bed where she would stick her blue gloved fingers so far up me that I wanted to literally punch her! As if I had the energy to. I wanted to ask her what the heck was she doing and what would that solve. She was very dominating, and I didn't like her at all! For some reason, I couldn't build up enough strength to say a word. I remember barely whispering to my husband holding my hand saying, "She's hurting me" with tears rolling down my face. It took everything out of me just to say that as slow as I could so he could hear me. They had me plugged up to all types of monitors, and nurses surrounded me in numbers. Everyone was just moving so fast as these bright white lights were glowing in my face.

Next thing I hear once she released her fingers out of me was, "Baby doesn't have a heartbeat, and mom is bleeding!" I was so numb that I couldn't even register any of that! They immediately rolled me up to the floor where I would go into surgery. Once I get up there, there was the anesthesiologist telling me their 'gonna take care of me. Right after that, to my left was my doctor who had finally arrived. I'm sure he had to be woke up out of his sleep because it was now about 4:00 in the morning. I'm sure this caught him by surprise as well, because we were just at our last appointment to see him and everything had been fine. We even had the scheduled C-Section dated for Thursday of that week and here it is now Monday morning and this suddenly happened! He reassured me as well that I was going to be alright, and he would take care of me as he patted me softly on my shoulder. They rolled me back on the stretcher to begin the procedure by prepping me first. My doctor told my husband he couldn't come back with me, and he was pretty upset. He had been able to come hold my hand any other pregnancy, so he didn't understand the reasoning for it.

Next thing you know, I heard my doctor and apparently another doctor discussing where and what should be placed. I mean just a normal conversation. I prayed they didn't have any trouble putting me back together again. So, I guessed everything was about over. I never heard the cry of my baby, and they hadn't yet brought him into me like usual. I think right after that I just dozed off again and thought maybe when I woke up, everything would be back to normal. Well, I awoke to a room full of people just standing around which were family and friends. Everyone looked so dull, and no one was talking or anything. As I looked over slowly to my left, I see a guy holding up some kind of clear hollow tubing moving it up and down. Then, I saw my baby with just a blank stare and a tear that just rest on his face. I still didn't know exactly what was going on, but I just dozed back off to sleep again. I learned once all the drugs had pretty much wore off that my uterus had ruptured, that they had to resuscitate my baby to bring him back to life and were headed to Kosair because he was having seizures on his brain. The cause was deprivation of oxygen when they had to resuscitate him. I didn't think too much of that registered with my soul, but what I did know is I had to get out of this hospital and go to my baby.

The next morning my doctor explained everything that happened again. I originally was supposed to have my tubes tied right after the baby was delivered but that wasn't accomplished. The doctor explained to me that I had lost too much blood when my uterus ruptured, and he had to get consent from my husband not to perform a tubal ligation. They needed to close me back up because the risk was too great. I already had to receive a blood transfusion as result of the loss of blood. When he got done, I begged him to release me so I could be with my baby. God answered my prayers, when everyone else thought I was crazy including my husband. They felt like all my body had been through that I needed to heal from the inside out. My husband was going back and forth checking in with the doctors and sitting with the baby. He came back and would tell me everything that was going on with Joshua to all the medical lingo. That was all good and dandy, but when it came to my baby, I needed to see him for myself. I was released within a day and a half and couldn't wait to hold him! We arrived at Kosair Norton's Hospital. I tried walking on the elevator, but my husband stopped me immediately and got a wheelchair! My doctor made me promise him that I get a wheelchair once I get there. I just felt a little sore, but didn't think I needed a wheelchair. When I arrived on the floor with my husband pushing me in the wheelchair, even the staff was looking at me with stares. So, I'm like what is going on. I guessed they were surprised at the fact I was there so soon and just had a baby. I get up out of the wheelchair and lean over to see this innocent little baby hooked up to all these tiny black wires. His head wrapped with white bandage around it to hold everything in place. He had wiring to monitor if he was having any more seizures, and if so how often. I couldn't even hold my precious baby, but was just so happy to see him.

That next day I came to the hospital, I would get to hold my baby. He was 6 lbs. and a bundle of joy! He also had to be on a breathing machine again because of the deprivation of oxygen he lost. Just as long as he got healed while he was here, we could all go home together. For 2 months, we would make several trips back and forth to the NICU. In the midst of all that going on, he also had to have surgery so he could eat. When they had to revive him, he didn't get that chance like any other baby to swallow. So, Joshua had to have a gastrostomy tube inserted so he could eat. When they released us, the doctor's main concern was if he needed to be on oxygen at home. He had a couple of complications while in NICU with shallow breathing at times and had to have the oxygen turned up. They eventually decided that he didn't need any oxygen to be sent home. But, they did send him home with a suction machine, which he had to be suctioned every 20-30 min and or as often as needed. Ok! However, I'm just excited we're leaving and ready to start this journey.

We arrived at home with all these kits and devices. From the tubing devices to feed him with to the big suction machine that had to be emptied every time we used it. And not to mention, it had to be cleaned thoroughly so it wouldn't smell. As much as I couldn't deal with anyone else's mucus, it was time to click into reality. Life in this precious baby was vital, so I dealt with it! Although the nurse absolutely warned us when we came home just to take our time and get organized, otherwise it would be a disaster! She was never lying. That it was! I didn't even know where to begin or where to put anything at. My husband would soon have to return to work on 3rd shift. I must say there was plenty of long nights and mornings. I'm not sure how I slept with having to suction him almost every 30 minutes. Between suctioning Joshua every so often and emptying the suctioning container, cleaning around the stoma so it wouldn't get infected. Then preparing and feeding him yet alone taking care of 3 other kids at home which was going to be really hard for me. Someone even mentioned to us about applying for FMLA. My husband checked into it, even though it took a while. He had to continue to work full shifts until everything was approved. I'm not sure if that was a good thing or not! Of course, my husband helped but he also had to get his sleep as well working 3rd shift. I still was confused why they didn't send my baby home with oxygen, and my thought was will he get suctioned forever and how will that work. I wanted to go back to school, but I knew my life was at a standstill. I couldn't possibly work at this time, and to get a disability check would take months to receive it. All the bills were on my husband, and here it is I had this beautiful Camry sitting in the driveway but couldn't even afford it now. I had to give my car back. There was no sense in my husband trying to pay my high car note and his as well. Well, what could I say at this point! I could only give it to GOD. Thank God after several weeks, my mom offered to give me her truck which was a 98'Infiniti Qx4 with no tint! Just factory tint on the back windows! LORD knows I've been changed! Here it is I'm actually riding without tint! And the car wasn't quite up to date. I had to be grateful because it was free!!! Eventually we put money after money in that car, then one of the running boards came loose and was just hangin'! It was so embarrassing! I mean it would hit the ground as I was driving over a bump at times! The horn would just blow periodically without me pushing on it! We finally had someone rig up the running board, but they end up having to take it off. The kids would say, "Mama, you know it's time for a new car, this is raggedy!" I told them we were 'gonna ride it till the wheels fell off! My middle son said, "But mamma your wheel did come off!" I said, "Well, until the other one comes off!" Can we say, "Humility comes before honor!" My Dad and husband wanted me to get a new car, but I refused to let us go into debt with a car payment! I've learned. Until we were set and I knew I could trust him not to gamble any longer, then I possibly would consider it. Over 300,000 miles on it, and I was still rolling! I gave GOD praises for my 'old faithful' truck! I know that was one of the ways GOD had to humble me even more…….

I loved this baby with everything in me and so did my family. He was a miracle baby if you asked me. Joshua had literally passed away from the time I felt his last kick getting out the truck. Then, we had to wait for my doctor to arrive and for me to get prepped and ready for surgery. While all this time, his little lifeless body laid in me. But GOD had another plan that probably even the doctor wasn't ready for. But, I must say I still had a lot of questions for GOD. Like, "Why couldn't you just allow him to breathe on his own 100% and to swallow then everything else could get better. And why did my uterus rupture after having such a perfect pregnancy for almost 9 months and a healthy baby? Was I not supposed to take my husband back or was I not supposed to have sex at that time? Did that trigger a reaction to make me have contractions? I mean, what do you need out of me GOD and what is the purpose out of all of this???"

Well, my husband took Joshua to the doctor, and they said he might have a case of cerebral palsy due to the oxygen loss. His hands did start to ball up at times really tight. I knew that wasn't normal but dared not to believe that it was that. I heard the crackle in my husband's voice. He was hurt to hear that. I think we both denied it and said they didn't know what they were talking about. We knew we were praying for GOD to heal Josh and allow him to swallow first and foremost. I was at the grocery store when he called me and was on his way home. He said that the suction machine needed to be charged, and that he needed to suction Josh. I asked if he was turning blue or having shallow breathing. I even told him to meet me at White Castle since he was coming this way, so we could at least plug it up to suction Josh. He was just so snappy and said he would just meet me at home. So, on top of the news about Josh, I guess he wanted to take his hurt out on me. Well, I flew home because now he's in his feelings, and I had to make sure my baby was okay. Not that I was afraid he would let anything happen to Josh, I just knew I needed to get home asap!

I pull up at home and hurry to get in the house to suction Josh. He then says he would be back. Then when I questioned him, he got sarcastic with me. Josh was about 2 ½ months old, and he calls himself leaving again. Now I truly thought that with us having this baby in this critical shape that he wouldn't dare walk out now. He sure did. Now I tell GOD I see why some of this might have happened. You are really showing me, but I won't listen huh GOD. He stayed gone for at least a week maybe and what I thought was 'gonna be the hardest time of my life doing all this by myself. It was by far that, and it was the most trying, but yet peaceful time for me and the kids. Although he did come and get Josh just one day, I was really ready to quit speaking about divorce and put it in action! If he would leave me in such a time as this, then he wouldn't be able to withstand through anything harder than this. Pastor Malone had just preached a sermon, 'Kill it before it kills you!!!' I had already made up my mind after that powerful sermon! I walked with my head high determined that following Monday I was going to the Family Court office for a divorce. There was 2 African American men sitting in there. And after I filled out everything I needed, I walked pass them and said, "My Pastor said kill it, before it kills you!!" They just shook their head agreeing saying, "That's right!" It never seems to amaze me about me! My words really ain't nuthin! They have no power whatsoever, because I'm not acting upon anything! I'm not moving any mountains with the Power that GOD had given me!!!

He came back home and apologetically said how wrong he was and that he would do better. I laid down my expectations once again and life went on. He was still working at Tyson Foods, and FMLA was still in the process with his job. I think he wasn't really worried about that job, at least he all of a sudden seemed like it. While he was still seeing the chiropractor, something just didn't set well with me. I remember my step-father saying he never wanted any blood money. I used to ask my mother what that meant. He was referring to if he ever got into a wreck, he would rather have his health rather than to get paid. What good is the money if you don't make it out alive or you have a severe injury for the rest of your life! Money can't take all pain away!   I thought about that with my husband's lawsuit, going to the chiropractor and him not even being hurt. I had a talk with JESUS and expressed my thoughts. He told me to tell my husband that if he got out of the lawsuit, he would heal Josh! I had to ponder on that big time! I had questioned GOD on this one! "Now GOD, you want me to tell this hard headed, self-centered, spoiled, prideful man to drop everything in exchange for his son to be healed?" I mean, he loved his son and all, and I'm positive he wants healing for him. His faith is not there like that, and I'm just not sure if he would believe me! And if he knows it's not a guarantee Josh will be healed, then I would think he wouldn't want to take a gamble on losing his money! Well, I was surely obedient and did what I was told to do. He got a little quiet. It seemed like he was thinking about it, so I left the rest up to JESUS! I did wait a while and even got into somewhat of a dispute. I argued the fact of why he would continue going through the lawsuit knowing there is a chance our son could be healed. Eventually, he stuck with his final answer and continued with the suit. That really made me wonder what kind of man I married. The verse 1 Timothy 6:10 (KJV) reads: "For the love of money [that is, the greedy desire for it and the willingness to gain it unethically] is a root of all sorts of evil, and some by longing for it have wandered away from the faith…." speaks volumes and it is the WORD at that! I just moved on with life like I knew I had to.

I still was confused about the hubby's hours and how sometimes he would either come home late or real early. I received a letter one day from Tyson Foods. Of course, I immediately opened it up because I already knew something wasn't right. The letter explained how my husband had not been to work for a while now, and that the union was giving him a chance to write something stating the reason why. I am pissed! First off, wondering where in the heck has he been every time he said he was going to work! This is insane, so the nights he came home early was when he just was too tired to keep up. I remember some days he came in with a terrible headache. The deceitfulness caught right up with him! He walks in that door and acts as if he worked a long shift. Sitting down on the couch and falling asleep, but really he is playing possum! Boy quit it!!! I nicely asked him how his night was at work and then showed him the letter. He read it, and had the nerve to say he didn't even know what they were talking about and that he's been to work every day he was supposed to be there. I went off! I told him, he better tell me where he's been at or it's over for good, and I meant that! I needed access to his portal at work to view hours and days! And on top of that I told him I needed every paycheck stub from the start! Trust was out the door for me!!! Those papers were getting extradited right to the judge immediately! After all that lying, he finally admitted he was on the casino boat. I'm looking at him crazy as all outdoors! Yea! That's an easy way out! But yet, I told him he is wrong as 2 left shoes and that wasn't acceptable at all! The excuse was because I'm not working, so he had to bring in extra money. I asked him where his faith was like he had before, and what happened to trusting JESUS and knowing that he will supply all our needs just like HE did in the beginning! But instead, he never did take the opportunity to write his job back to even explain why he was absent those days. Well, they end up sending a final termination letter to the house. Welp, there goes that great job and benefits too!

So, now Joshua is about 4 months, and he is a joy to have! I just dealt with the fact that he was the way he was and just continued to pray for healing. It was 'gonna be what GOD allowed it to be in the end, and we would still love him regardless. One thing I know for sure was GOD had to be really watching over me and protecting Josh at the same time. It was plenty of nights I'm sure I slept for a long period of time like my body was used to, and Josh needed to be suctioned. One night after I had fed Josh and gave him a good bath, he laid in his bed right beside me. He had been really congested for a couple of days and now on top of not being able to swallow. Could you only imagine how that felt, less known a baby? So, I laid him beside me and just loved on him. He always had his eyes open looking up, very seldom did he shut them. As I laid in the bed, I simply asked, "GOD, why would you let a baby suffer so much and not just heal him?" After that, I reached over and opened up my Bible, and there I saw how GOD heals in different ways.

After reading some, I must have just dozed off. My oldest son came in the room that next morning to tell me bye, which was ironic. Usually, he just walks right on out the door assuming I am sleep. Not sure what was different this morning. I turned over to fall back asleep, but smelled Josh, so I turned on the light to change him. His face looked somewhat clammy and his eyes were closed shut! I screamed and just started crying, then I started to shake him to see if he would move, then picked him up and placed him on the floor in the living room to give him CPR. I called 911, but they could hardly understand me because I was sobbing so. They told me an ambulance was on the way but to continue to perform CPR. My baby didn't budge. The first responders rushed my baby to Norton's Kosair, and I followed in a police car. I called my husband's job to tell him something had happened and to meet us at Kosair.

Once I arrived, they had my baby laying there and told me they tried resuscitating him. But GOD sought otherwise, my baby was gone. Soon as my husband walked in and saw him lying there, he literally just fell to the ground. I couldn't move and wasn't going to! I left him exactly right where he fell. I know it sounds harsh, but here it was my baby was gone. I needed to hold on to him as long as I could and wasn't letting go. Not to mention, I felt like he could have been healed if my husband had listened to what GOD told me to tell him. But he didn't, and my emotions were at a high. But yet, I still had this sense of peace, and I knew I couldn't think about that at the time. As I sat, cried, and held his hand, his body became colder and harder. At that point, I knew his body was a shell and knew his soul had already gone to heaven………..

Chapter 5

Same Ole Story But Different Script

Some months later, I wanted to try and get my life back on track. I really wanted to evaluate me and get deeper with GOD to know the purpose he had set for me. A couple of months after, I scheduled to take the test to get into nursing school. Well, I failed that test. I just kept working in a lab processing those specimens. Not really where I wanted to be, but just doing something until GOD sought otherwise. My granny stopped by, and I guess you could say she cheered me up. She hadn't really seen me since Joshua's memorial, but we had talked on the phone. She pulls up, and I greet her from the porch. She looks at me with this strange look and says, "Guuuurl, you look like DEATH standing on a bus stop sucking on a lifesaver." Yep! That's my Nanny that has no filter!!! Of course, I laughed at my Nanny, because I just wondered where and how in the world did she just make that up! I thought that was pretty considerate compared to what she said at Joshua's memorial. She stood over his little beautiful precious body while he lay in that gold casket and said, "Well, I be da**, he looks better in that casket than he did when he was alive!" LORD knows she is the only person that can say something like that! I agreed and said, "Yes ma'am, Nanny he does!" At that point, it was better to agree than to disagree! Love her dearly! That was her love language and wouldn't exchange her for the world!

Back to my job where I met some really great people, it seemed as if everywhere I worked I was able to share the Gospel with someone who needed it. That was so amazing to me. I tried to read on my lunch breaks when I could. Unfortunately, I still didn't have any transportation. My poor truck had broken down, so my husband had to either drop me off to work or I would drive his truck. Thank GOD for my grandmother coming over and watching the kids while we both worked 3rd shift. That was the only shifts open for both of our jobs at the time. So, on the days he was off, he got to the point where he would ask if he could gamble at the Casino for a couple of hours and come right back home. At first, I agreed because I knew he was going to try and sneak to do it. He took me with him one day to a house poker game in the garage to prove how long he stays there. I was ready to go within 10 minutes. He begged for us to stay because he had a good hand. I had even called houses he was at before to see if he was still there, and he would get on the phone. I guess he thought that would make it better. I must say, he is very good at the game, but at the end it still doesn't pay off. Once that money wasn't enough, he would start hanging around the same friends who lived that lifestyle. Which is that fast money life! So, here it is trust is all the way broken again! Furthermore, I really didn't know where he could be; even though, he did stay on the boat and or at house poker games for several hours and a lot of times until the next morning. I drove all the way from my job out LaGrange, because I couldn't possibly believe he was still at the boat. Surely he was sitting right at the poker table with a hat on and looked half sleep. He couldn't even get the kids off to school, because he kept saying he was coming and never did.

Then, when I would call him and he had to answer, he claimed he lost every time! I told him that the devil was a lie and that story is a bunch of foolery! It didn't take long to see the occurring problems in the marriage fast! Then, came another set of the friends from the past which were living the same street life like back in the day. We would have plenty of arguments about him hanging around his friends. He would say he was strong enough to be around them and not do the same things they were doing. Of course, he said I was acting like I was his mama! I said, "Nah I'm not acting like ya' mama, because ya' mama would let you get your way!" Then he would say, "I know I got off probation some months ago, and here it is you, actin' like my probation officer!" I was used to those same lines, but yet I still stayed on him! I wasn't 'gonna let up either!

Low and behold, he continues to hang with his friends that meant him no good! Except it began to be more of a constant thing. So, now it's the casino boat, hanging out with his friends and trying to make some extra money! So, as you know there wasn't any time for us, and he had to hear what he calls nagging every time. Now don't get me wrong, when we were good, we were good! He knew how to take care of me, home, and the kids! I would notice every time my husband read his Bible and went to men's Bible study that he was just as humble and content. But once he put that Bible down, it was hell to pay. Two of his friends that he was hanging with everyday got locked up, but my husband didn't. Praise be to GOD, and he knew GOD was looking out for him and spared him another chance. I would tell him how good GOD has been to him and that HE was giving him every sign and a way out each and every time! I knew my prayers were being answered! So, I must say he quieted down his ways for some time. Now that he's jobless from a good job, we both prayed so hard about. He did find a job down the road working 3rd shift. One morning, I just so happen to call the job because his phone kept going straight to voicemail. He usually would be home by now. So, I called his job and they said he never came in for the shift. He answers his phone and of course denies the fact that he's not at work. I'm like. Oh! Wow! He lied again! I told him I called up there. Then finally he claimed that he did leave early and went on the boat. I still told him I didn't believe him, so he put some random country talking guy on the phone to tell me he was really there. We shouldn't even be having this problem, because when I let him come back the last time he promised to never go on a boat! What in the world is going on now GOD! This is a disaster! I know you have ups and downs in life and marriage, but all these lies and not being trustworthy is insane to me!

So, I need to address these issues, get answers and communicate about everything before it gets deeper. Of course, he doesn't want to talk and shuts down. Every time he would still walk out, I would start to have to answer for him. When the kids came home and asked where Daddy was, the parishioners in the church and family members, especially when we had family functions. For the most part, he would come back by then but not always. I never was ready or prepared about what to say. And quite frankly, it began to be the same story. The more I told it, the more scripted it sound except this was my true-life story! He was still in and out the house over the course of our marriage. It got to the point that I said to GOD, "Okay I'm ready to go through with the divorce!" I can't tell you how many times I walked my little tail up to Family Court Division and never would end up going through with the divorce. But, I still had the divorce papers on file because I asked them could they not file them yet because I was still uncertain. I knew I would probably never get him to sign papers again. I already had to have him do that in order to get back in. GOD knew my heart wasn't ready! I was still thinking there might be a change. I mean, after all, I did say I do. But it was beginning to seem like 'I' was doing all the work, but not as a couple.

I figured my husband needed some friends who were accountable, and would hold him accountable for his actions. I had already introduced him to a deacon in the church who was just a little older than us. He would call and remind him of Men's Bible Study or any other event the Men were involved in. One deacon even payed my husband's way to a game they traveled to. I loved the fact they cared and were involved in his walk with GOD. So, my husband was introduced to a man in the church who were mutual friends with another man. The man moved closer to us, and asked my husband could he help him move. My husband did and actually began to be good friends with him. I was glad he had some godly men to hang out with, but my husband started to spend too much time with him. We had a big argument one day, and I even asked him what the heck are ya doing down at his house! That set him off. He knew I was referring to something negative! I had to ask myself and GOD was I insecure within myself or felt like I lacking something. Even on one Sunday afternoon, both the men in the church called to see if he wanted to come down. I'm thinking here it is a Sunday afternoon, we have kids and things we could be doing! That man has a wife and the other man has a life! He took off walking down there, and I was pissed!!! I waited and called him some hours later and asked if he were coming home soon. I sure didn't think he would spend the whole afternoon there! That following morning, the man from our church, who just got married and just moved in not far from us called. Well, I had got in the shower and walked with my towel on to the door where my husband sat on the porch. Here it is the guy from our church. I spoke to him and then gave my hubby a look for not letting me know we were having company. I walked back to my room and put my clothes on, and walked towards the door. I see something being passed from one hand to another! I stepped out on the porch in disbelief! I mean I couldn't even talk at first I was so shaken up! With tears falling down my face, I told that guy, "Why in the world would you be coming to this house first and foremost and disrespect this home! Here it is my husband is trying to get closer to GOD, and I thought you would be encouraging him to do right instead your passing blunts to my husband!" I also asked him how he would think the Pastor would feel about him doing something like this! He seemed to not mind and even told me that I needed to stop trying to be somebody's mama! I told him to leave our premises immediately and looked at my husband to see what he was saying! He is actually getting on me and really upset! It looked like his eyes was just shot red like the devil! I don't know what was all in that blunt, but I have never seen my husband get to that point and holler! He walked away angrily as well! Screaming, "I'm not his PO, and they not even on him like that!" I was so hurt, because all I knew was I needed to protect him from people like that and try my best to stop the enemy from attacking! At least if I could help it, I knew where he was trying to go and that was to have a closer relationship with CHRIST! So, he was new at being a Christian, he was still on baby food and hadn't reach solids just yet. So, I wanted to be that Shephard of the house on that spiritual level until he could! I didn't want him to think that it was just okay especially on a Sunday afternoon after church to just lay back and smoke! If that's the case, he was going to love being this kind of Christian! I just knew I wasn't delusional about all that hanging around. And what's sad, is that it did start off with my husband coming home reading verses that this man had shared with him. Like I explained to my husband, even if that guy had a problem with smoking, as long as he was at least seeking help to stop smoking but that didn't seem to be the case. But to just boldly come over to our home and rub off the very problem that I was hoping that my husband would get delivered from. Iron sharpens iron period!!!

It is now almost 4 months after my baby has passed away, and I go to the doctor because I'm not feeling normal. I knew I just couldn't be pregnant that quick and my uterus ruptured on top of that. The doctor comes out to tell me that I am pregnant! I am in disbelief and shocked at the same time! How could this be and my body is still healing I would think. The doctor explained to me that my uterus was like sewn back together. I thought, 'Oh my goodness,' here it is my marriage is in a disarray, and I'm just beginning to figure out my life and this happens. Guess I won't be getting a divorce now; although, I know GOD wouldn't put more on me that I could bear. I really felt as if HE would take care of me. At 5 months, we go for the ultrasound and the nurse tells us it's a girl! Now that was an exciting and grateful time in my life. To think that GOD would give me double for my trouble, and entrust me with a baby girl. Especially after going through such a life challenging moment, yet here I am! YOU are surely worthy to be praised! Not that I ever wanted any kids after my first two, God again thought otherwise. I will forever be so grateful!!!! My doctor of course scheduled a C-section 3 weeks prior to my due date to decrease the chance of my uterus rupturing again. 12 months total from losing my Josh and 7 days apart from Nov. 22nd when Josh passed to Nov. 29th that following year, I birthed a healthy 6 lb. little girl. 12 is faith in the Bible and 7 is completion. I'll take those numbers!

A couple of years go past and same thing but different situations! Here I go talking with my GOD again! I know HE is sick of me, but, I had to tell him that I didn't want to be stuck in a marriage for years and not be happy! I see that way too often in people's marriages. Then, I will look up one day and life will pass me by just because I began to be too complacent in a situation which I call "learned behavior!" You get too comfortable with all the wrong things going on and not even trying to fix them! Both parties have to agree on change though! We sought counseling from our Pastor's wife, and it was great having a 3rd party to look forward to meeting with weekly. I knew that I could talk about any and every problem I had, and my husband would more than likely have to respond. She wanted to introduce some techniques for communicating which I knew that is what we needed. I was so excited about learning these attending our next session! Everything was going pretty good or so I thought! When that day arrives, he comes out the blue saying he is not attending any more sessions and that I know her all too well! Really! I nicely packed up his bags for him this time, and I didn't even give him a chance to walk out! Because I simply set expectations that I had for us and the marriage, and that was to attend marriage counseling! That was his only means of getting back in the house after walking out several times prior.

I knew I had to start focusing more on GOD and give HIM my problems and concerns about my husband. I was way too focused on him! He would even say some time, "You can't change me. You have to let GOD change me and quit worrying about me!" I just wouldn't listen. I figured he really doesn't know what he is saying! But oh well, I'm going to still try to direct my focus on being active in our church. Time and time again, leaders of the ministries including my Pastor would urge the parishioners to get involved. He often asked, but I had been sitting on those pews for years letting it go through one ear and out the other. I figured I didn't have any gifts to offer. I didn't want to have to deal with any more kids than I already had. Needless to say, I joined the Usher's ministry and loved it! Not long after, I joined the Children's ministry as well. I must say there were times I didn't feel like teaching and attending meetings, but as I grew closer to GOD I enjoyed it more. That ministry was life to my soul and the kids! I learned more about the Bible more than I ever knew! It also took less focus off my husband and gave me peace for the most part.

So, shortly after me putting him out he gets an apartment. I guess he knew I wasn't playing this time! The papers were signed and all that needed to be completed was parenting classes. By us having younger kids together, all of us had to take classes in order to complete the divorce. Well, it was like tooth and nail trying to get him to pay and attend the classes. He wasn't going to do it! As a matter of fact, 2 months after getting the apartment, he wanted to come back home. This time I told him he would have to call the church himself and explain to the Pastor's wife why he never attended another session. And also explain to her that now all of a sudden, you're more comfortable with us talking to a man from the church and someone who I didn't know personally. And that he did, but he still couldn't come back home just yet. In the meantime, he gave me a key to the apartment and he still had to pay both our mortgage and his rent. If this mess wasn't just as crazy! I told my granny about it. Yea the one that doesn't have a filter! Her exact words verbatim were, "You don't have to keep walking on egg shells around that ugly a** nigga!" Oh my gosh!!!!! I knew my granny had it in her, but I didn't at the same time! I never laughed so hard in my life! She put it pretty rough, but it was the truth! Now she loved my husband as well did my family, but she didn't like all those disappearances he pulled. I would feel like, I bet not say this or mention this because next thing you know he is all upset or leaving! That went on for years, me not being able to express my feelings on any issue, except for times when I was just fed up and then I would get out of order! Meaning try to pop him so hard with anything I saw! Knowing I used to be ready to fight a man back in my days, he really wanted me like that! Every time I would go off, I felt convicted!

I mean one time he made me so mad that I tried to push him, and guess who falls! I mean an ugly fall, ME!!!! GOD!!!! How is it that he is all in the wrong and you allow him to keep getting away with murder? He came in one other time and said he was going to get us some Indi's chicken. He had us waiting for over an hour because he went back to that street life and was taking care of things he shouldn't been taking care of! I had told him on several occasions that I didn't live that street life anymore, and that I wasn't going to allow him to bring that life into our home! When he came in that door, as hungry as I was I knocked everything out his hand! He walked straight out the house, and who was left to clean it up! Me! The floor was so sticky, and now I was even more pissed because I wanted to eat those peg legs off the floor! I was so hungry! Again, it all falls on me! Everything that had occurred in our marriage had just taken a toll on me! And the result from that came bitterness and anger towards him often which was not healthy at all. As Sunday started to draw near, I didn't even want to go. Walking in church became a conviction for me, I couldn't just go in there lifting up my hands and praising HIM with the same hands I just threw chicken with. And use the same tongue to worship him, and here I just told my husband some few choice words. Most of all, what kind of example was I showing my husband who was a fairly new Christian. That was hard for me, so I knew I had to go about it another way. Even times when he would shut down and the kids could tell as well, instead of being bitter I started back fixing his plate. When I would serve him a plate, I remember my eldest son asking me why I fixed my husband a plate and that he didn't deserve it. And my response was, "Son, you have to overcome evil with good!" I explained it to him through Proverbs 25: 21-22 KJV "If thine enemy be hungry, give him bread to eat; and if he be thirsty, give him water to drink: For thou shalt heap coals of fire upon his head, and the Lord shall reward thee." Once I broke it down to him, he said not a word. Thank you GOD for that WORD!

Needless to say, we both went to counseling, and he participated as well. But, this time I had already told the counselor and my husband that if this didn't work, I was done! He gave us homework assignments and told us if ever a time came up that there was a disagreement, to discuss a time later and pray together. This was probably about our 3rd session when we met with him. HA! HA! We tried it, at least I did! When that time came to pray, I asked him for a time and he didn't want to follow by the assignment. When he gets in those grudges, he won't budge! He wouldn't even set a time to pray or come back later. I couldn't wait to meet with our counselor again. It was like I was a kid waiting to tattle tale. It truly was, because I knew I couldn't talk to my own husband about any issues. Unfortunately, he had to skip a week and we both agreed to the following week thereafter. That morning came for us to attend counseling, and he already had an attitude for some unknown reason. I reminded him of our appointment, and he said he wasn't going! He made up the excuse that he wasn't aware of the new date. I also reminded him that he knew that was a promise he made and there wasn't any backing out! He was very adamant saying he had to go look for a job. I explained to him that our counseling is only an hour and is essential to our marriage and that he could go right after that. He basically wasn't budging and said he wasn't going back. I said so again you played me, and making me look like a fool! Knowing that was one of the stipulations for him coming back! I had to be the one to call him, but you're the one won't go. He told me he didn't know what I was 'gonna do, but that he wasn't going. That really proved to me that he didn't want to make the same sacrifices that I was willing to make. I didn't dare look GOD's way because I knew he was sick of me once again! I should have known again and again this was going to happen! The bad thing is that he is the one who called to set it up. LORD JESUS! PLEASE TAKE THE WHEEL!!!

I looked up and within a blink of an eye, we were going into our 6th year of marriage, after saying I didn't want to be complacent in my marriage years prior, but just continue to allow myself to settle for anything. Not to mention the kids seeing this behavior and thinking it's okay to just walk out on mommy and not be respectful. Here it is I have a daughter now, and what would I be teaching her as a woman. Somehow, a whole lot of time passed and the counseling issue thing got swept under the rug. He knew he wasn't in good standing with me and that it wasn't going to last too much longer. I began to just get quieter and basically just not give a care.

My cousin was getting married on a cruise ship in a couple of months, so he called himself surprising me. The Cruise would also stop in the Bahamas as well. I guess maybe we needed this 'us time' and to get a break from life itself. We were so excited until I was so late trying to rush and do my daughter's hair before we left that we missed our plane. He had the whole trip planned and paid for. I felt so bad that he had to pay for another 2 plane tickets. Because there were no more planes going out that day to Florida, there was no reimbursing for the tickets. Then, we had to sleep in the airport, because we didn't want to miss it at 4:00 in the morning. Let's just say we talked, laughed and had a ball in spite of everything.

Once we actually touched down and rode a shuttle to the Port, we met up with our other cousins. We were in seventh heaven once we boarded the ship, it was so beautiful! We get off the elevator and low and behold there was a Casino! Oh LORD!!! Now don't get me wrong, I wanted both of us to enjoy ourselves. I actually thought that would be the last thing on his mind since he played it so much back home. So, we had to set some guidelines about the Casino from the jump!

Chapter 6

You Can Lead A Horse to Water, But Can You Make Him Drink?

So, the first 2 days he really didn't piddle in there long. But that next night, he promised me he would only stay for an hour and no exceptions. I mean we were all dressed up, and they were having a formal dinner that night. I came back up to the casino where he sat, and I kneeled down beside him. I said not a word, but was hoping he would glance over to say okay here I come or something to the affect. I finally tapped him gently on the shoulder, but he never responded. So, I waited a while then whispered his name. He turned around so fast, looked down at me and said, "WHAT!"

I said, "You know they're going to shut down the dining room soon!"

He responded, "Okay! You see me gambling!" I was in awe! I didn't know whether to smack the dog sh** out of him or walk back to the room like a little puppy! Cause that's what I felt like! Grant it, I did just that! I thought to myself as I walked back to the room, 'Does this n**** really want me like that! I will go back to KEY-LO-LO in 2.2 seconds and have this n**** on suicide commission! He thinks he can disappear. He wouldn't even find me on the map! Now he can try and google that!' See! That is how quick my flesh would rise up within me! I was furious, but more saddened than anything.

As I laid down on the bed, I moved his pants to the side. But, heard something move in what felt like a container. Only to find a prescription of tabs. Apparently, he was still getting this medication from the chiropractor he'd been seeing which he says he's in pain and needs them. No wonder he's so short-tempered and numb to my feelings and his. Which was not surprising at all, but it just seems like a new situation every time! I just laid down and cried not even a bit talking with GOD! Because you know what, GOD is so sick of me! Same ole story and yet not doing anything about it! All I could say is, "LORD forgive me!" I know I'm wrong, but just keep allowing myself to settle for just anything. I hear the keycard swipe, and I quickly dried my tears! He said, "Come on! And as soon as I get done eating, I'm going back to gamble!" He also said because I interrupted him, he didn't get to finish and that I got him all off track so he lost some money. I'm the blame for everything!!! I actually got up and went with him to eat. We sat at the table, and I mean there was pure silence. I even tried to spark up a conversation despite me being so hurt! He sat there and didn't mumble a word! Then, the tears just rolled down my face. I was so glad my family didn't show up. I was still embarrassed, because other couples were around and I'm sure wondering how I could be crying in this type of atmosphere. He looked at me and said, "What are you crying for, what's wrong now?" I then looked at him and said, "I'm just not happy!" I couldn't even eat, and you would have thought he would have been somewhat remorseful. When we got up from that table, he surely did go right back to the Casino for the rest of the night. I called myself staying out enjoying myself! I refused to go sit in a room just because of his attitude. For once, I will make me happy and take care of me!

When I arrived to the room, he was already asleep. I pretty much made up in my mind that I was done after this trip! On our way home in the airport, it was like he came back to life and talked about how we have to do better in the marriage and ways we can fix it. I thought to myself, does he just get in these moods every blue moon and a light bulb goes off? I just don't get it! I feel as if sometimes I'm right there with him. Because he's turning me on and off just like his feelings are my feelings. But to keep down catastrophe when hubby wants to talk, you better talk because you don't know when the next time he'll talk again.

It's coming up on our 7th year anniversary in a couple of months. I had already said to my husband either we're going to make it or we're not. The number 7 is completion and I refuse to go another year and nothing get accomplished. He surprised me once again and booked a trip to Las Vegas. It was much well needed, and we did enjoy every bit of it! He talked about some areas he wanted to improve in. The following day, I'm wondering why he hasn't come home from work yet. I get a phone call hours later from a correctional facility. My husband gets locked up for a charge back in 2004 that we thought was taken care of. He originally got pulled over for the limo tint that I've told him to take off several times. They ran his name and apparently he had a warrant. How ironic that was. I mean all of us including his mom were so confused. They let him out in a couple of weeks, but he ended up losing his new job in the midst of it all. The judge set a court date to appear in the state it originally took place which was just an hour and half away. Well, by him losing his job in the meantime, he was still back in the world doing worldly things. It seemed like it was getting more frequent that he would leave. While he was out of the home, his court date came to pass and he missed it. Fooling around with that boat and everything else, the police caught up with him and locked him up. He started getting into the WORD and even spreading the Gospel to other inmates. He had younger boys who had committed murder talk about how they didn't have a father figure. My husband was in shock and start to cherish his life and family. But, I'm still at home with 4 kids and doing it by myself. Really it was no different when he was out, because he would be playing poker. My husband is a very spoiled child. So, between his mother and grandmother, they wanted him out of there. My father-in-law was going to put up the money to bail him out. He was even willing to give his tithe money! I thought, "Ah nah!" So, my mother-in-law and I went up there. Soon as I stepped out of the car, something didn't set right with my spirit. I expressed to my mother-in-law that this wasn't right and that GOD doesn't want him to get bailed out. I explained to her that this charge popped up for a reason and it's not by happen stance. She agreed, and we both got right back in our cars. Of course, my husband couldn't understand it, but GOD knew what was best. I knew because I heard from Him, but still no one really understood. Because he didn't bond out, he was shipped to another state to take care of that 2004 charge. When he would have people call me from jail, I could hear the change in his voice. He said it was rough and his blood pressure shot up detrimentally while he was in there. I knew this is what he needed to take his life serious and to be the Shepherd he needed to be for the family.

He was released, and we were joyful! I mean me and the kids were happy to have this new changed man home. Thank you GOD for change! They did put him on probation for that charge. My mom said, "If that isn't just stupid!" Holy Ghost spoke to me real fast, and I told my mom "No it wasn't, because apparently the good LORD wanted him on probation for a reason." My mom said, "Well yea, that could be true."

My husband was determined to make a change this time around. I heard it and was seeing it. My husband joined the choir and everything! Parishioners and even our Pastor was so excited to see him up there singing. I invited his family but wanted it to be a surprise! We were in Bible Study and the Pastor called on him and ask him what this particular passage meant to him. My husband's exact words were, "I'm just learning to be consistent with GOD, but I'm riding his coat tail and I'm not turning back!" I knew for a fact GOD had given my husband a change of heart! He's not even the one to just be prepared to talk like that in church. That set the tone, and I knew this was a new beginning for all of us. He wanted us to renew our vows and even went to my family get together to get on one knee and ask me. I felt pressured to agree, and also I didn't want to embarrass him. Even though I felt like I had been embarrassed almost my whole marriage. And not that I didn't want to, but I just needed to feel secure, safe and be able to trust him that he wouldn't let us down again. And now I see what his mother meant! Again, it wasn't long before history repeated itself! "Now GOD, I really am confused! This time my husband did some things different in life, and he was getting closer to YOU, and now what has happened????"

As I picked back up typing this book this afternoon, LORD knows I wanna give up, but I know that's not in my destiny! While walking over here to the library, oh yea that's another story. I'll tell ya' about that later on! The Holy Spirit was speaking to me while going through my circumstance! I'm getting tired myself of typing the same line about my husband coming and leaving! I know you all reading this book are tired as well! I know ya' cussing and uh fussing and calling me all types of choice words as I am myself probably saying, "If she lets him come back one more time!" Guess what? I'm saying the same thing as I'm typing! How foolish of me to continue this over and over again! But, I have to keep pushin'!!! Thanks for allowing me to vent, I needed that! Now back to the story, just a lil' commercial break! THANK YOU HOLY GHOST!!!!!!!!!

My husband went to report to his probation officer one morning, at least that's what he said. Whenever he walks out with a slight attitude he ends up somewhere else. He calls me to ask, "Where is the proof of insurance?" I asked what was wrong, and he said he'd been in a car wreck. I'm like, really again! This time only someone ran into him! He wasn't a bit upset, because he knew the process and what was in store! So, yes my husband gets into another car wreck! Yes! I know this sounds crazy, but it's real! And first thing I thought was, 'He is lying!' It was very true! So, no work because it will interfere with the early appointments to the chiropractor. Of course, he could have worked a later shift, but chose not to. He was still waiting on this major company to call him back. He had already taken the physical the day before and drug test. This was a really great job and advancement was there. I was grateful for the support. A teacher at my daughter's school's husband worked there, and I asked her about a referral. She said, "Okay, I'll ask my husband when he gets another one." I said, "Good and thank you!" Well, within I know a month, she passed it right along to me! I was ever so grateful because for one, she nor her husband didn't know my husband personally or his work ethics. For two, nobody has to be generous and it's a blessing when they are. After a couple of months, my mom asked a lady from my church that she knows if she could check on the status of the application. Again, we had never spoke to this woman only saw her at church but knew of her son. We received a phone call within a week for my husband to take the test! Look at GOD!!! You betta show out!!! I think I was happier than he was! So, that was in progress because he had passed the written test.

While waiting to receive a call from this company about his other test, he was continually seeing all kind of doctors saying he had a shoulder injury. Heck! I didn't know whether he was telling the truth or not! His whole attitude changes again and back to the boat he goes for hours and hours! I'm so over it!!! He claims when I make him upset, that going to the boat calms him down and relieves the stress. Yeah okay, any excuse will do! All I know is there are hotels on the boat all day long, so the trust is out the door for the one hundredth time! And our trust ain't built like that!!! I don't care how many people I hear in the background! When there was no success there, he came back in town to the local poker tournaments. He told me if I couldn't support what could be his passion, then it wouldn't work! I told him that I knew GOD had better things in store for him and that he was so much smarter than just settling trying to take a gamble on these dice. I dared him to take a gamble on GOD and be consistent with it! He of course wanted me to sit back and see him live out his passion of gambling. I told him that I wouldn't be able to stand by that! He texts me saying that he was throwing in the towel, and that I'm not there for him in supporting his passion. I text him back saying, "The kids and I have been there since Day 1. We have sacrificed a bit much for you, but for you to walk out several times and leave us! Yet, we still love on you every time as if you had never left! I always picked back up the pieces where we left off! Basically, starting brand new and just forget trying to fix what happened in the past, so we wouldn't have that challenge in the future. And or know how to fight it next time a situation comes up with the WORD of GOD! I knew I had to pick up the CROSS and follow JESUS! I knew it was time, past time at that! Way overdue for way too long! Eight was new beginning and another year could not go by, and I not make a conscious decision! This had to get serious for me and my kids! Either me and my husband was going to get on 1 accord or not!

It has been a month since he's been gone on to his dream of being a professional poker player or what have you! This has been the longest he has ever stayed gone. He's out with his friends and brother almost every day having a ball! But, mostly his brother just going from here to there and everywhere. It was the norm for us, but still hard as a mother. My son is now 17 years old and loves the ground he walks on. Of course, he's been knowing him ever since he was a baby. At least he used to. I believe he didn't respect him as much because he saw the in and out over time. My son is wanting to be grown so fast and it was surely coming. He's getting to the point where he is now talking a lil' slick and walking out the house when he gets distressed. Wow! Oh LORD! What have I started? A history that could lead to a tragedy! Especially the way the world is today. This takes me back to when I was watching a sermon of T.D. Jakes' a couple of years ago. As the camera came near, it was like he was right in my face literally talking to me! I recall him saying something about, "You have just enough time to change your children, and your children's children." And that's all I can remember him saying. So now some years later, I'm thinking is it too late? I continued to allowed my son to learn from my mistakes. And now he's doing what only he saw being done in this home, but yet he knows it's wrong because he has said it before. I know I had a part in this as well. Although I thought I did something a tad right when I didn't allow him to come right back in, but yet eventually he did return.

So, while my husband's still wandering in the world, he gets a call. A call from a guy who wants him to work out of town assisting with the hurricane in Texas. I thought, "Well dang. He's gone again on another break and doesn't have to take care of any responsibilities! Then, he's inviting all his friends and his brother to go. I already know that's 'gonna be a disaster! Oh! And he was so hyped up too! I just don't get it! "GOD, do you see what you're doing???" There goes my mind all over the place again! I had to really sit back and think! Well, he is talking about sending money home to help with the bills. And it's not like he's been home anyways, helping out with bills a lot or even with the kids! So, what do we have to lose! I mean, it seems like he always gets a way out! He's still waiting on a settlement check to be sent and only giving me bets here and there if he wins at poker! He's only getting the kids every blue moon, because he's too busy in the streets. Again, I was worried and putting too much focus into my husband! As I talked, my mind is now at ease! I expressed my concerns to my father-n-law about it, and he said it's not going to be a vacation for him and that they are going to work them hard! And that there won't be much time for playing around! Needless to say, it seemed as if it started out like that, but there were smoke sessions going on and everything else! People getting sent home and some not even having work! And a job that was supposed to last for 3 months, only last for a week and a half. Guess I was a little upset at first, because I got over the petty stuff and was focused on him sending home that money! None of that now! We were a little excited of him coming back home, but now what? And he wasn't in the house before he left! So, does he just get a pass to be back home again! So, since he didn't make the money he thought in Texas, now he saying he has to make up for it. He made it in the house for about 2 weeks, and there he goes back to the hard knock life!

The next day, I checked the mailbox and it was the letter we been waiting for! More like I was waiting for, he seemed to not be anxious! I went ahead and opened it up, so I knew to tell him when the start day was. The letter read that he failed the drug test! Woooooow! SMH!!!! Like the saying goes, "You can lead a horse to the water, but you can't make him drink!!! " I called him to let him know. And oh, did he say that was a lie and that he hadn't been doing anything! I truly see why some people don't like helping people get employment by using their name as a reference. This is the kind of stuff that happens! And funny thing is that he just got upset over someone he'd known to get him in on a job. Well, what's so funny is once my husband arrived, the lady told him that the person didn't really want to hire him. My husband couldn't understand why the guy even told him about the job in the first place, and so was I! I had to really think about it, and now I see! Your character, morals, and integrity are everything and can take you far! This was so embarrassing. Here my mother and I vouched for him and people went out on a limb for him, but yet he failed! I can promise you I won't open my mouth nor help him get another job. He will be on his own as he likes to do anyways! And that it was the results of the tabs from when he was prescribed when in the car wreck. I politely told him, "That's a lie, and you had already taken the drug test before the car wreck." He begged to differ. So, I told him the letter said, "You have about a week to appeal it, but they have to use the same sample!" Let's just say it never happened! I'm like my husband's cousin who already works there said, "How do you pass a drug test for your PO, but not for a job!!!" I believe at times, GOD will block certain things in our lives, inspite what everyone else may feel that they are getting away with. He has a plan and a purpose set for each individual in due season. You may be delayed in your blessing, and or maybe you couldn't handle it! Along with many others of GOD's reasoning and or timing! That's what

I love about my almighty GOD. He is a just GOD even when the odds are against us!

I pretty much asked my husband again about the seriousness of poker, and how he had made it a full-time job, plus overtime! I guess I wanted to see if he had a change of heart, because one night I happened to look out the window and there he was. He had apparently fell asleep in the car which he was known for doing. That means either he was taking a break from one gambling place to another or maybe he wanted to come in. With me, not knowing how long he was out there, I had to call and ask was he okay? It was like 2 in the morning! I called, and he answered. I asked him what he was doing and was he trying to come back home? He pretty much replied with the same story and said either I can roll with him or get rolled over! And I told him, "Well I guess I'm dead then!" It didn't take long for me to decide that I wasn't going to be a part of the foolishness! Again! Here I'm telling myself that me and the kids deserve better. I could no longer be bound and shackled down with someone that had not made up in their mind that they were going to follow JESUS! We had to be on 1 accord! We went on with our life as usual. I knew I had to be really prayerful and fast or something! I mean I have to do something different than what I had been doing! My life depended on it! I often thought that GOD was going to take me out of here if I didn't wake up and give him my all! Like the time my tire flew off while I was driving on the expressway. Thankfully we were okay, but we were on the side of the highway and didn't know who to call. Well, some guy pulled over immediately and asked did we need a ride, I turned it down. I went ahead and called my husband. He answered and came for us. Soon as he picked us up, he said his mom had called about his oldest son (my step-son) saying that his bag was packed and to come get him. How ironic this was that he comes to pick us up and this happens out of the blue. Well surely she had his bag packed, and we went over there to get him. Not sure why he didn't just drop us off first, because we were going home and my husband had been out of the home. I guess he assumed because he was picking up his son that was his way of easing back in. I was in shock like really and my heart began to hurt, like really hurt! I laid on my bed right after we came in, and I mean it felt like I was having a heart attack! Then I just dozed off to sleep, but apparently the Holy Spirit wouldn't allow me to really sleep. A voice spoke and said to me that I had to separate from my husband immediately! There was no mistake about it or no mishaps! I heard it very clear, and the next morning after his son caught the bus, I had a talk with him. I explained to him what had been revealed to me and I believe, he thinks I was jiving! At first he was in agreement, but later said I just didn't want his son there. I couldn't argue with him because I knew the truth! Not only that, I could only imagine the disagreements that would have taken place over my step son. None of our beliefs about discipline were the same, and what would he do as soon as something didn't go his way. He would be dragging his son right out of there. That was not healthy for him, and he had already been through life's troubles some beyond his control and I wasn't going to contribute to that! I loved my step-son too much to put him through any more unnecessary conflict that could have been avoided.

So, he left, and moved in with his granny. Because I was obedient, it was like that burden was lifted from my chest instantly! The sharp pains in my chest stopped as well. It seemed like we needed that, and I was willing to exhaust all options before divorcing. We still did everything as a couple, but he just went home at night and we agreed not to have sexual relations. We both needed a clear mind to hear from GOD on what we needed to do. Another sign I had was when I was asleep one night and it felt like I couldn't breathe. It felt like someone was trying to squeeze the breath out of me. I finally woke up suddenly! I didn't know what this quite meant, but I know it was a sign, confirmation and or something I needed to know or do. I would say some months later, my Pastor spoke on the demonic spirit of Python! He explained that it was like a snake squeezing the life out of you! I had to re-think that incident and what could have happened to me! I still wasn't complete on why that was, but knew I never wanted to experience that again. I had to re-evaluate me! Not my husband, because I've had too many losses throughout my life.

Chapter 7

God Redirected My Plans

So, I knew I wanted to get back to nursing school. I really didn't want to go back to a community college and finish my pre-requisites, but attend a college that was hands on and where I could grasp my career as I went. Someone had mentioned about a 15-month program to obtain your L.P.N. I visited the school and liked it. I told GOD, "If you allow all my paperwork and financial aid to go through, then I would go hard and not quit!" This time I was finishing and going to obtain my degree! I was finally going to do something for me and my kids. I couldn't worry any more about my husband. When I tell you within a couple of hours, I had everything processed and my schedule in my hand. I was truly headed towards my destiny, and the sky was the limit. Boy was it a struggle and numerable sacrifices were made. There is nothing easy about nursing school whatsoever, and it had been a long stretch of time since I had studied nursing. Most of the curriculum had changed, that's why I still beat myself up by not finishing my initial course work. I guess it's better late than never. Now, that I'm in my elder years, I wish that I had pushed through. I would have had about 18 years in the field of nursing if only I had stayed focused on my career. But, the streets and the material things in life had me caught up. Yet, I settled for a lifestyle that couldn't contribute towards a career in the future. Welp, I better not. Guess I could say the same when I stayed in my apartment for 9 years paying rent, when that money could of went into my home that I was going to own. Well, I better not dwell on the past for too long or time will continue to pass me by.

By this time, I had already finished a year, but failed some of my classes which delayed my graduation date. With my husband getting locked up and not being able to have a good support system was rough. I wasn't sure how I was going to get through the next quarter, because the times to meet would be even earlier and longer days. I had enough on my plate even when he got out, because I felt I needed him to help with the kids. There goes his way back in and not even deserving of it. Even though he did get the kids together and cooked dinner most days while I was pulling shifts at the library. A sistah was tired! But, I knew it was going to pay off in the end; although, I was a little concerned about my book getting finished. I expressed to GOD one day asking him how am I going to finish my book. I mean once I graduate, I'll be working 12 hour shifts most likely and will probably never get it finished. I would think I would be too tired to even lift a pen. I never really got an answer at that time. I just went about doing what I knew. I had this one teacher who was of African descent who taught by only power points whereas I felt more comfortable with a textbook. Needless to say, I put more focus into my other classes and figured there was still more grades to put in, so I would make it up. I just felt like I needed a break at this point. The distress was wearing on me I think. I figured if I go ahead and withdraw now, then I would have just that one class to focus on. I did just that, and it was more understandable the second time around, but still challenging. The end of the quarter came, and the teacher's posted the grades. Pharmacology to me wasn't my favorite subject, but real interesting to me! Everyone was anxiously waiting on their grade. I just said a prayer and left it there. It didn't take any time for our teacher to post the grades. Once I walked in the house, I checked for my grade and there it was! A 77%!!! I failed! It was like my heart shattered. I couldn't even express or have words to say. I kept refreshing the page, logging out, logging in over and over. This meant I could no longer be in the nursing program again, at least at that school. Not only that, there wasn't many schools that would accept my school's credits at all! And I have to pay back over $20,000 in loans, and yet I have no degree! Come on GOD, we have to talk! I made you a promise that I would study hard and finish to the end, and here it is I have come this far and failed never to return. I didn't even want my husband to know I failed! I felt like he wouldn't have anything positive to say especially if he was in a mood. I recall him sending a text days after I told him and it read, "All that time trying to figure me out, you should have been studying!" That moment right there hit me like never before! I felt like such a failure and here it is another attempt but no accomplishment. I tried to think of every reason why this time I could have failed. Maybe I should have taken advantage of tutoring or something. It was difficult to work in study groups, because I only trusted me. And look where trusting me got me! I was sooooooo sick. It just wasn't fair! What will I tell my kids? And what about when my 4-year old daughter asked me, "Mommy, you going to Clinicals today?" As she always did! All the sleepless nights and being away from my family was just in vain. I know I logged in 20 more times to see if my grade changed. It didn't change then. But a couple of weeks later, I so happen to see that I had an 80%. I emailed my teacher, wrote to the BBB and even talked with another administrator. They advise me to take further steps if I thought something wasn't correct.

Here was this passing grade I saw, and even they had me email them as well. No one could see the grade I saw apparently, how ironic! So, then all of a sudden one of the people email me to say that grade was from a previous quarter. All I wanted to know was how could that be. If that was so, I should have never had to repeat if I ever passed it! That never made a lick of sense to me! The only thing I know is JESUS reigns, and all I can do now is get still and start back from the drawing board. Maybe GOD is honoring the fact that I was concerned about me finishing my book when I had that talk. I still wasn't all the way sure, but I just started to type little by little. I had a long way to go. It took me some time, because I had to let this become reality. I was still so hurt, and this feeling wasn't going away anytime soon.

One thing I know is that things do happen for a reason. I know GOD has a plan. I just don't know which direction I need to head in now. And I know He will keep me in the midst of and order my steps if I just follow. I know what the devil meant for evil, GOD will use it for my good. "This had to happen for a reason GOD, but I just don't know why yet!" "For I know the thoughts that I think toward you, says the Lord, thoughts of peace and not of evil, to give you a future and a hope. Then you will call upon Me and go and pray to

Me, and I will listen to you. And you will seek Me and find Me, when you search for Me with all your heart." Jeremiah 29:11-13 NKJV I still had just one more small question for GOD, then I would quit my pity party. I asked GOD why a whole year and then this! GOD spoke to me, "My time is not your time!" I said, "Okay GOD!"

Well, back to my caregiving job which was the only thing I had to keep me sane at that time. I'm going to have to increase my hours now and find a better paying job. I can't depend on my husband because he's still not there. And gambling money I was not expecting, although, he will get that settlement check. I just hope he doesn't try to flip it playing poker. I was sleep one night and here it's the hubby texting saying, "I love you and miss you!" Awww! That was so sweet, I said in my mind! My response to his text was, "I bet you do. It's getting cold outside! LOL!" I turned back over and went to sleep. I'm just glad it wasn't a text saying something was wrong. Like not too long ago, he blew my phone up saying he blacked out while driving and went to the hospital where they said his blood pressure had shot up detrimentally. He misses that comforting mothering affection and love. Ain't nothing like it when you been running in them streets. We always would pray for him asking GOD to protect him and guide him. My prayer was to help him have a change of heart and not a prideful one.

One afternoon, our youngest son got off the bus, but I wasn't home yet so my neighbor got him off. Shortly after I came home, my son came running with the neighbor. My son said someone came over and left a blue note. It was a notice for my husband from his PO! I called him and texted him a picture to report on the date given, which would have been the following week, so that he goes into report. The phone rings, I answer and the voice the on the other line says, "You have a call from Louisville Metro Corrections!" Look who calls me, and look who had to go pick up the car from the probation office! Okay! So, I'm the first person you call when you get looked up, but the last when you out in the world! I figured for some reason or another he was going to forget that date to report. That or either he had to cleanse his urine. LORD JESUS! Same process but different time. So, I wonder why he would call a thousand times knowing the free calls are just a couple of minutes. You would have thought he was never 'gonna get to talk to me again! Well, he is right! Because my phone is not set up like that and neither are my pockets! After so many calls, I just quit answering. I'm sure he will be booked in real soon! And then if he still wants to call, he can get one of his buddies to call us. That's just how I was feeling. It's like aren't you tired of putting yourself and family through this! I had already made up in my mind that me nor the kids were going to see him in jail! That's what I told one of his church member's friend, after he asked me were we going to visit my husband. He told me, "Because that's your husband!" I replied, "He wasn't at home with us before he was locked up!" I still wasn't really bothered, but I still had a heart and of course, loved my husband. I would hate for him to have a heart attack or something happen while he's in there because of the stress. One thing I do know is that the last couple of times, his blood pressure shot up really high! With that being said, I felt some kind of responsibility for us to go visit him. It required hours just for us to see him and just the place alone was filthy dirty. I would have all kinds of gadgets for the kids to play with. In my thoughts, I just didn't understand why we had to take out time for him now. But yet he had all the time to spend with us when he was out. That didn't sit well with me at all, especially when the kids would lose interest in being there when being there for a long period of time. I really had to do some serious soul searching this time indeed! My mind was so all over the place about whether or not I should proceed with the divorce.

Off I went to the Family Court Division having intentions to proceed. The night before, I started having some chest pains again, the same pains from last time GOD was trying to get my attention. I wanted everything to go smoothly so that any little distraction wouldn't deter me. I drove around the building at least twice, now remind you I had about 20 minutes of spare time before I had to get to work. I'm talking to GOD the whole time, and finally I find a parking space which wasn't far. There was time already in the meter. I get to the window and explain that I have paperwork already on file. The lady gets the paperwork, looks at it and tells me that my husband would have to sign again. I took a deep sigh! I had mixed feelings. I was ready to get this over with, and okay it must not be meant to go through with this. Yet I explained to the lady that they told me everything was good, and they just needed the okay to push the papers through. Our divorce decree had expired, so both signatures had to be signed again so I thought. I told the lady he was incarcerated, but all the while I was quick to think this and that. She said it only had to be 1 person from the parties to sign. And so, I did! I walked out of there within 7 minutes, and got to work even a couple of minutes earlier. Now the hard part was explaining to him that this time I really did send the papers through.

So, the kids and I go visit the hubby. While waiting to see him, my heart was just a racing! I really wasn't sure how he was going to take it. We sat down and I hurried to tell him! I told him how I just couldn't do it anymore. It hurt me to my heart, but at the same time it was a relief like no other. His response was, "You think I'm 'gonna just let you go like that. You know we see it all the time on T.V. how people get back together and re-marry!" Well, that was a better response than what I thought! He was actually content and did understand that he has put us through a lot. He said he probably did need this to happen in order to see the light. Then I said so if those papers go through, then that is it for us. I feel like I'm still giving HOPE to something that should have died long time ago. I mean was I hoping for any other errors to happen so it wouldn't be FINAL. He even called later that day and asked was I really serious about what I said. I told him, "Dead!" We visited him that following week again on that Thursday. I told him, "Well, I guess you been praying, because I haven't received any papers yet!" My prayer was still, "LORD, if I made any mistake about going through with the divorce, then please GOD block it how you see fit!" That next day on Friday afternoon I checked the mail and there it was! I slowly yet anxiously opened up the envelope and it read that the divorce was

FINAL!!! Oh, my goodness!!!! I must say it came as a shock and didn't know if I wanted to cry or what! Then, I had to immediately go into prayer, and thereafter I knew everything was going to be alright! "For GOD has not given us a spirit of fear, but of power and of love and of a sound mind." 2 Timothy 1:7 KJV That verse is what I needed to get through each day. Yea! I know right! Quoting that verse sounded really good to me too! But truth be told, I still questioned GOD! I just wanted to make sure I didn't miss anything. That following Monday I called up to Family Division and gave the lady my name and asked the lady, "Does this really mean that we are divorced?" The lady responded without any hesitation, "Yes ma'am! This divorce is FINAL as of December 11th!" LORD JESUS! It hit me again! I said to GOD, "Okay I was just checking!" I couldn't do nuthin' but chuckle! I know GOD just looks at me so foolishly at times and says your head is so hard! I had to give HIM praise, and consistently thank Him! Also, to allow me to accept that the divorce was final and give me the strength and peace I needed each day.

I had already explained to the kids, and they took it well. It is so amazing how JESUS will give even your kid's peace about a situation that seemed bigger and too hard for me. But, I still have to tell my now ex-husband! That sounds so strange but it's sure enough real! My father happened to be in town that weekend and wasn't leaving until Monday. The kids didn't want to go for some odd reason. So, just me and my father went, because he wanted to also put some money on his books. We go in there and my Dad sits down and talks first. I'm standing up behind my Dad just smiling, but I see he is just looking serious and not too happy. So, I told my Dad he could just wait outside the door for me. I sat down and I told him that the papers did go through and the divorce was final. As he looked down almost the whole time, he told me he appreciates all I have done and that me and the kids don't have to come up there anymore. He said he just wanted to get his mind together before he gets out. I let him know I respected his wishes. I knew that the divorce had weighed on him. But to tell you the truth, I felt like once he got out he would be just fine. Nobody had really heard from him for about another month. I did attend the court date, and he winked at me and I blew him a kiss! He still didn't get out! Nobody could even understand why he was still there or why he hasn't been picked up to go to the other state. His probation officer even said that everybody is stupid, and she didn't know why he was still sitting in there. She had made every call she needed to. In the meanwhile, he did call the lawyer about the settlement check and gave them permission to let me pick it up. What a blessing that was, and I took care of the bills.

While he was still incarcerated, I needed to get my mind together as well. I put more time into my book that I needed to get done so I can help save people through JESUS CHRIST! GOD told me that the same amount of hours I put into nursing school, I need to put into this book. Thank you GOD!!! I was hitting up the library every chance I could. Even on the weekends, I would go to New Albany library and let the younger kids get on the small laptops and bigger kids do their thing there. We spent 4-5 hours on the weekends there and didn't have much time for anything else. I knew I had to sacrifice some things in order for GOD to fulfill his purpose for my life. I heard it too many times, like on the radio and through people I would meet. If I turned on the radio, there was Steve Harvey saying motivational things about life and how to go about things business wise. I started listening to 94.7 which was everything to my spirit especially in the morning on my way to work. I felt like I still needed more of GOD! So, I started to fast so GOD could reveal to me and speak to me what part I had in the world to contribute. I also knew my ex was getting out, and how I needed to go about doing things as far as him. I knew I had to let him know there could be no late nights and definitely no staying the night. I had to learn this new way of living and still be sane.

Look who pops up at my door!!! My ex has been released! My middle son literally jumped up in his arms. They were so happy to see him! He had all these plans, but I knew I still had to wait on GOD for whatever next step he wanted me to take! It was time for me to start plunging forward to my destiny, because I am tired of leaping. My focus had to be on getting me together, because I spent too many years focusing on him. He found a job and would go home to his mom's every night as planned. But during the day soon as he got off, he was with us. Everything was pretty kosher. I can deal with this. Even in the morning he would come over before he went to work, and we would read our Bibles. It is so funny that our 5-year old daughter knew the routine, so when he would walk us in the house she immediately said, "Okay Daddy bye!" No sugar coating over here 'cause the world ain't going too. I had already sat down previously and explained to the kids why daddy goes home and clearly we're divorced. Our 7-year old asked me, "So if Daddy gets married again, will I have another mama!" I immediately said, "You will never have another mother!!! She would be your step-mother," I told him. I walked in the other room to tell the ex what our daughter had said and low and behind here comes our son. Now, he's asking questions. Their dad explains to them that he would never marry anyone else but me. I was shaking my head and told him don't tell them that. My ex said, "It's the truth. I said, "But still, we really don't know the future. I didn't want our children being told one thing then another thing happens. That's been done in the past way too much!"

Well this night he hadn't left just yet, so I went ahead and got in the shower and actually debated what pajamas I should put on. I knew to pick them out wisely, but I said, "Oh well, we can't do anything anyways." I must say I put on the most fitted pajamas I had, and there was that voice telling me something but I sort of tuned it out. I go in the living room, and we sat and watched television. It really was past time for him to go, but he had dozed off. So, I go over and sat close to him and then sat on him like a friendly sat. SMH! I did a throwback I guess you would say, and we sort of clothes burned. I thought, 'Oh yea, this would work!" I mean we're not actually having relations until I began to have those chest pains again! Okaaaaay GOD!!!! I hear ya! I hopped up so fast! I thought I was going to have a heart attack! I said, "Okay honey, I'm sorry! I shouldn't have provoked you like that. It wasn't right at all." And I told him that should never happen again, and we called it a night! I had to ask for forgiveness and thanked HIM at the same time for convicting me! That could have easily led somewhere else and thank GOD it didn't. And it never happened again either! It probably wasn't 3 weeks, and he went in grudge mode on me. This is why I know we had to have some space. I couldn't continue allow myself to linger on that path of destruction any longer. I had to be persistent in what I truly wanted for me and the kids. The very ordeal God delivered me from, I kept prolonging my advancement in my spiritual walk. If that's the case, I would have to re-write my story but the ending might not had been the same just for my disobedience! Now I truly know how you can love someone enough to let them go. And if it's truly meant for us to be, won't a devil in hell be able to block it!

"Are you ah'ite???" My oldest child and his friend used to say that all the time to people. It seemed corny at first, but I really had to ask myself, 'Was I alright???'

Chapter 8

Trust God and Do Good

Why GOD saw fit to save me from the average Joe not allowing me to be on drugs or get addicted. Or why I'm still in my right mind through all I've been through, but yet my childhood friend who was just as beautiful as ever and had long beautiful hair, now has hardly any hair and weighs about 300 pounds because of a mental illness! I was the 'wild child' and the disobedient one. She had such a quiet demeanor and all, yet, GOD was still preserving me through all my mess! I had another childhood friend I went to school with and caught back up with her in my latter years through a mutual friend. She had 5 kids and an exceptional occupation, but had a guy who was in that lifestyle. She ended up marrying him but also ended up with cancer. She went through chemo the first time and it left, but unfortunately returned. Our mutual friend told me she couldn't understand why she was the one who developed cancer. I actually made the assumption that she felt as if he was the one living the worldly life, but yet she had 5 kids and obtained her nursing degree. Unfortunately, she passed away due to the cancer. I remember standing by her bedside apologizing for not being there as much as I should have. I prayed with her and asked GOD to heal her if it was in HIS will, and I told her to ask GOD for forgiveness for whatever she needed him to forgive her for. I felt like I could have been a part of all of those situations! But GOD!

I tell you what! GOD is so amazing! When I had my abortions and was so uninformed about everything, GOD knew my heart! Not saying that I would get out of any consequences! Oh no! That's just not how that works! You better believe I had to suffer for the choices I made, but at the same time GOD held my hand through it all and would not let go. He actually could have very easily just took my life! Just like I took HIS unborn children's life regardless of the awareness that I did or didn't have. But thank GOD he doesn't repay evil for evil or allow our dysfunctional choices to measure up to his consequences. If so, I would have been in trouble! One day a young lady I'd known had to make an emergency visit to the ER because of some unbearable pain. Once she arrived, she was informed that not only did she have blood clots, but was pregnant as well. The doctor strongly advised her to terminate the pregnancy. In other words, she was advised to get an abortion because her and the baby's lives were at risk. I didn't think too much of it until I went there the day of and low and behold, EMW abortion clinic. LORD JESUS! Not back here again! I am so against abortions ever since I received the appropriate knowledge about the whole process. So, I showed the lady my ID and sat down next to the young lady. I just so happened to look over at the other door way across the room near the entrance door and see a girl standing there. She was actually inside the glass door. I walked as close as I could, saw her hands moving up and down and she was crying. I assumed she was explaining something as she was talking to someone on her cell phone. I start waving my hands to get her attention asking her to come around to the other side. She wasn't really hearing me and kept talking. I started praying asking GOD to show up in her life, help her to make the right decision and know that GOD will be there with her through it all. She finally came around to the other side, and I was able to talk with her. She explained that she had 5 other kids and didn't know how she was going to do it. I gently explained to her my story and how we laid down, made those babies and it just wasn't fair for us to end their innocent life. I mean it's fun when you're going through the motions, but you have to take responsibility if that time comes. I couldn't express enough to her how GOD was going to take care of her like HE took care of me! I made it clear to tell her that the road wouldn't always be easy, but if she had a change of heart it sure would be worth it! I also let her know that GOD would honor her decision of keeping her baby. She was still not so sure. So, I just gave her my number and asked her to please call if I could help her in any way and told her that I would be praying for her! While that young lady walked back in to finish the process because she had already paid half her money, I went into deep prayer! I mean I was crying and all. At the same time, I texted the young lady who had already went back and I was hoping she wasn't already starting the procedure. I texted her a long message saying to trust GOD and to take a risk with JESUS! 'I know what the doctor said, but HE has all the answers.' I told her to remember when my uterus ruptured and how they sewed it back up, yet I was pregnant just months after that. I could have had an abortion because of the risk of that happening again, but I knew it happened for a reason and that I was going to trust Him and HIS plans. While I kept looking at my phone for a response, I never received one. I continued to pray for both young ladies and left the Clinic. Once I arrived to my car, a text came through and it was the young lady I had talked to who had the five kids already. She said she decided to keep her baby and thanked me! You don't even know and never will know what that was like for me! I just boo hooed! I mean I just thank GOD and gave HIM all the praise that had been due!!!! Needless to say, the young lady I initially came there for actually went through with the abortion which would be for medical reasons per her doctor and she agreed. May I say that some months later, she was became pregnant again! I almost didn't believe that she really stayed and went through with the abortion. She must have literally conceived some weeks after the abortion, and didn't want to tell me because I had sent her the text telling her to just trust JESUS! And may I say, she delivered a healthy beautiful baby! I know what I know what I know because GOD kept me and showed me! And all I had to do was have that faith as small as a mustard seed. I had another encounter where someone called me about how the procedure went. Except, I gave them another procedure of how it went and that was GOD's way of doing things! She already had an older child and didn't want to start over again. I explained to her as I did the other young ladies at the clinic to trust HIM and take responsibility. Also, that usually you end up getting pregnant within that year again. She made the right choice and had a beautiful child that she just loves and adores today! Another incident with a young lady, that I'll call my little sister, became impregnated. Her mom felt she was too young and wouldn't finish High School and graduate if she had the baby. But my lil' sis wanted to keep her baby. She came over to my house distraught because her mom was forcing her to go to the Clinic the following morning and have an abortion. Because she was underage, she had to be with an adult. So now, I was responsible for getting her to the abortion clinic. Mind you, her mother wasn't aware that she wasn't with me. As I dropped her off across the street from the EMW Clinic, she met up with her mom. I proceeded to pull off, and her comes my lil' sis running towards me across the street in White Castle's parking trying to hide in between brick buildings. I was scared myself especially when I heard her mama say, "You little B****, I'm 'gonna beat your a**!!!"

Next thing you know, she hopped in my car screaming, "Come on! Pull off before she comes! She 'gonna kill me!!!!!!!"

I sped off so fast, and thank GOD the Second Street bridge was right there! Thankfully and eventually, her mom let her keep the baby with some family members convincing her. I guess I can say I had a part in that decision helping to kidnap her child in a good way! Afterall, why not re-visit my old stomping grounds that can and did have such a powerful impact on me and others!

I know I can't undo anything in my past, but I would sure like to give back to the world in any way possible that would have a permanent and positive effect. Especially with my kids, just like my parents did! When my mother used to go to the NCO club where the army men would be, I used to ride with her to the park near there. I would always watch my mother. It was meddling more back then. But I recall this one particular man I did like for my mother, and he would come visit. One day, my mother was on the phone hollering saying she didn't know he was married! My mother immediately ended that unhealthy relationship, and I never saw him again! I'm sure by me remembering that call even though I was so young, I believe it weighed on me in a good way! Probably the reason why I have never committed adultery! My mom always told me it would bring on health issues as well. The same was my Dad having an impact on my life, and us walking through the grocery store when I was about 11 years old. A guy came up to my Dad and asked if he wanted to smoke that night. My Dad's response was, "Nah! Man! I have a little gurl now and I don't do that anymore!" I remember it like it were yesterday and have told this story several times.

My Daddy didn't need a temporary fix, but a more permanent one. One that was everlasting, a GOD who was sovereign and who could turn his midnight into day. Lastly, know not to give up but persevere because joy comes in the morning. That is what kind of man he is today because of HIM! Now I'm glad to share it with the world. My Dad was short of slow, even when he grew a closer with GOD. My Dad and I visited my cousin and I ran into a girl I knew. She called my name to come over to her car. She had a trunk full of I'm sure stolen merchandise. My Dad was way across the street, and when I left the girl my Dad was curious even though I didn't buy anything. He asked me why I had even surrounded myself with that girl and explained not to even associate with people doing those kinds of things. As I grew older, someone brought some clothes to me in a garbage bag for the kids. I refused to accept it without hesitation. Even though the kids truly needed some summer clothes, that wasn't the way we were getting them. I have never been approached since, and I will stand for something and that is the morals I've been taught and integrity!

I feel like when both of my parents made the decision to be serious about GOD that it would eventually trickle down to my sister and I, but boy did it take a while. If only my mother could tell the story alongside all the people who witnessed it. Of course, I don't remember how mischievous, is the word I would like to use, I was back then (Laughing). Everyone, especially in my church, reminds me how disobedient I was as a child. But one thing for sure is that I know people were praying for me, and the prayers of the righteous availeth much indeed! Just like my mother, I would write down different verses, study them and write goals down. I will tell you this, she prayed for a husband in detail, a home to be built and to not continue working at the factory job she had. All of those things came to pass, and I was able to witness for myself. By me being so caught up in material things and outside appearances, when a good man came I shot him down. Before my mother was married to this man, of course they dated. His first appearance was not the best appearance. He came over in this white Sandford & Son truck, this plain t-shirt and some LA Gears! That's what did it! But, little did I know how important he would be in our lives. He was a working man and most importantly a godly man. My mother told me that one day he was in the basement and held his hands up high looking up to heaven. My mom asked what he was doing, and he said that was something going on out there in the world that apparently had something to do with us kids. My momma said, "Well tell me what's going on, I have kids out there!" And my step-father said, "So do I!" Although my mother never knew exactly what was going on, we knew he was interceding on our behalf and it was detrimental. It seemed like he was here for only a short time, but made a huge impact in our lives.

He passed away in their home on the couch chair with the Bible in his hands. My mom had been married to him for 7 years which means completeness and achievement. Of course, my mom especially couldn't even grasp why GOD would take away something she had prayed for leaving her living in this big house by herself. In which, eventually helped many teenage kids get through their difficult life as well as helping my mom with hers. We will understand it better by and by.

All these different encounters I've experienced has had a major spiritual impact on my life and has brought me to a closer relationship with my LORD and SAVIOR. Although, I know I will continue to face many trials and tribulations, yet I'm aware I have to persevere and stay trusting HIM! One word that has come to mind while I tell my story is "IDOLOTRY!" Meaning worshipping the sun, moon, stars, powers of nature, hero-worshipping, idol worship and etc. It can also be to have an extreme admiration or love for something or someone which brings me to 1 Kings 18:21 NKJV "Elijah came near to all the people and said, "How long will you hesitate between two opinions? If the LORD is GOD, follow HIM; but if Baal, follow him. But the people did not answer him a word." Also, I thought about 2 Kings 17:41 NKJV, "So these nations feared the Lord, yet served their carved images; also, their children and their children's children have continued doing as their fathers did, even to this day." That reminds me exactly what I have done all these years. I went from worshipping money to basically my husband. As much as I hate to say that as if he was some GOD, but really I did put entirely too much time into the kids and my ex-husband. That is like worshipping an idol because I put less time in GOD's presence! Every now and then I would take my problems to GOD, not purposely but just not thinking Christ-like. I sang, "Let go and Let GOD" a thousand times, but still wasn't doing that. I would have talked to a drunk or even a mute man on the streets if I could have about my marriage. If only I knew how to sign, I could see me now! I'm telling you that I'll be looking like a choir director!!! Just trying to find answers from anyone but GOD. I'm not sure how sometimes I would go to HIM, but other times I guess I thought GOD was tired of hearing my voice. Especially knowing I was going to do the same thing, or what my reasoning was of why I didn't go to HIM. I would talk to people just to spark a conversation so I could get confirmation and answers. Even though I really knew the main thing I had to do. I kept trying to understand why it was happening, and why he would leave. But, I came to find out when he was gone was those times I drew closer to

GOD, prayed more and got on my knees more. It wasn't so much of the husband, it was me, not being able to focus on GOD and give HIM not some, but all of my problems. I've seen it work, but I just wasn't consistent about going to GOD in prayer. Too caught up in my emotions, feelings, and the trials which would never change because of the way I went about things.

I recognized that as I was typing the issues I had with my husband and that I had to keep retyping. I kept changing the words and just all out of order, it was like the game scrabble. But as I started to fast and pray, GOD just gave me the most graceful words to write and I felt so much at peace. It's like the words rolled right off my tongue. As I became closer to the end of finishing my book, the more I grew closer to GOD and I must say fasting helped me so much! I never knew how much I needed HIM until now! I was fooling around on the internet and saw a chance to enter into a Christian contest. I was really excited, and was thinking that this was a chance for me to get a free publishing package. I was not even half way finished with my book yet, but felt like since it only required 4000 characters that I could do it. I had already mentioned to GOD if I didn't win, that I would be okay. So, I submitted my story after trying to sum my whole story down to 4000 characters. It took about 2 days for them to decide who had won, and they said the person would receive an email who won. I patiently waited on that Tuesday for an email, checked it and was not chosen as a winner! May I say I was crushed!!!! Even though I told GOD that I would accept it and be okay, it was the exact opposite! I said okay, "Help me Holy Spirit!" The devil is a liar!!! Then I thought, "I don't have to win a contest!" I'm winning for JESUS. Matter of fact, I've already won because I had been redeemed!!! And this was just a small platform to push me even farther! I'm trying to make disciples through the way I'm living and writing this book! And after that I didn't look back!!!

As I begin to wrap things up, I'd like to say I really thought I had all the answers just because I was the one not smoking marijuana and gambling! One very important lesson I learned in my marriage is that, "YOU CANNOT CHANGE NOBODY!!!!!!" AND as one of the marriage counselors told us, "YOU HAVE TO START WITH THE MAN IN THE MIRROR WHICH IS YOU!" It took me almost 8 loooooooong years just to get that! JESUS!!!!! I also learned that when I kept my mouth SHUT, I saw GOD personally work things out in my marriage, but that was only for a little while! I NEVER stayed quiet long enough to really see the VICTORY!!!! GOD gave me every sign, but

I didn't see it then because I was so caught up in judging his wrongdoings! I wanted and needed GOD to take care of him, even if it was just getting a spiritual whooping! A real hard one at that! I mean I talked so much that I know for a fact GOD allowed my veneer to come out! Yes, veneer I said! I know, my Dentist persuaded me to get veneers instead of braces because of my underbite. By him giving me a huge discount, I was all for it. And as you know if you've ever had veneers, then sometimes your tooth underneath won't be as white especially over a long period of time! Yea! I know right! Imagine that! Didn't it pop right off, and that literally was the death of me! I'm the one that talks and smiles a lot, and for GOD to just do that to me was heartless I felt! I even told my husband at the time, "Why haven't none of your gold teeth came off, you the one that does wrong!" He said with this a smirk on his face, "Baby, maybe GOD is trying to tell you quit talking so much!" I was heated! And yes, I eventually was convicted that this was all GOD's doing! He will do whatever HE has to do to get your attention, and HE knew that would do it! When I knew I could glue that sucka right on, I surely did! But, the trick to that was I still couldn't talk too much, because I was afraid it would fly out of my mouth! I dare not say any words that begin with certain letters like "F." That would have me pressing down just a tad too hard on my lower lip. So, I had to be very careful and gentle with my words if you know what I mean! Every chance I was giving GOD praise thanking HIM for my teeth and apologizing and repenting! Whatever I needed to do to make things right with the ONE that could supply my needs to get another one put in! Then HE made it to where the insurance wouldn't cover it and the bills wouldn't even allow any extra monies to pay for another one! I told God, boooooah you something else GOD!!! I told HIM I promised that I would be quieter and to just convict me when I needed to shut up! Naaaaaah! That didn't help either. This went on for another 2 months or so. I just began to deal with it and made up in my mind that GOD will fix it accordingly, and that was based on my actions and obedience. HE wanted to fulfill HIS promises even through a situation like this. I mean I had to take off the veneer when I ate, just so I wouldn't swallow it like I had dentures or something! It was such an inconvenience. I recall one time at my client's house, my veneer literally fell in the sink down the drain. Oh my gosh! I had to explain to my client with tears in my eyes and begging GOD for us to find it! Okay GOD! I get the verse, "Humility comes before Honor" my LORD!!!! You should of saw my client's 80 something year old wife and I trying to take loose the plumbing. She sat a bucket under there for the water to go in and low and behold there goes my veneer! Maaaan! When I heard that thing hit that bucket I shouted for joy! I told her I will forever owe her and thanked GOD! A couple of weeks passed and her son was off this particular day, and we just laughed as we told him about what happened. He had a similar story and said he had a temporary tooth on and actually swallowed it while eating a hamburger. He asked me did I want to know what happened next. Of course, I did. He explained he had to dissect his stool to find his temporary tooth! I said, "All naaaaaaw!" That's just crazy as all outdoors! Needless to say, after all that, he never did find it! Now, do you all wanna know what happens next??? Of course, you do! I lost my veneer again and couldn't remember where in the heck I placed it! My husband and I plus the kids looked outside and all in the house from top to bottom! Never found it and I was sick!!!!!!! I asked GOD again what I did to deserve this!!!! I've tried to be obedient and quieter as possible! I was determined to find that veneer. I called my dentist again seeing if I could set up a payment plan or something! They suggested I get a crown so that it would hold this time which was hundreds of dollars! For some reason, they wouldn't even do that. I was just in complete disbelief! I started to google ways to fix my tooth. I said to myself, 'Heck you can fix everything else on YouTube, so surely I can fix mine!' I got down to the nitty gritty and had no other choice! I was tired of looking like Felicia off the movie, 'Friday!' After countless times, trying to find my veneer, I had one last option. So, do you really want to know what happened next? Low and behold, I ended up with a similar story line as my client's son and needless to say, I never found it. Okay GOD!!!! Again! I give up!!!!! What in the world do you need me to do????? I had to get really good and humble to hear God's voice about what He would have me to do. Let me say with great honor that God provided in His timing. I was finally able to get another veneer even though I had to pay $1320. I asked and He provided in due time so I won't complain!!!

Oh! How I have enjoyed writing this book and hope you were tremendously blessed!!! This book is definitely not a pity party book or for someone to feel sorry about the things I've been through! My point was for you to see a partial part of my true-life story with the trials, tribulations, and testimonies! Hopefully, for someone to prevent a lot of these things from happening to them by being obedient to GOD, just hearing HIM and following HIS commandments! I really am just trying to share my story and allow JESUS to use me as a vessel to do HIS work so that He will get the

Glory!!! I feel like I would just be taking up space here on Earth if I'm not trying to help myself and others get to HEAVEN!!! I just don't believe GOD is just going to keep allowing us day by day to live any kind of way. Not being involved in our churches, giving our 10%, living a life that is giving Glory to the kingdom, committing adultery and fornication, telling lies, using our tongue to praise GOD, yet cursing and cussing each other. This is not living a life without flaws because of course none of us are perfect, but just trying daily to DENY OURSELVES, PICK UP THE CROSS, AND FOLLOW JESUS! That's if we are serious about having a closer and consistent relationship with the Lord. Then we can experience 1 Corinthians 2:9 KJV, "But as it is written: Eye has not seen, nor ear heard, nor have entered into the heart of man the things which God has prepared for those who love Him."

So, when I used to say I wrote the playa's book and published it, now I can really say with honesty, I wrote this book! But this is the LORD's book, and I'm helping change the WORLD!!!! "FROM THE STREETS TO A SAVIOR"................

THANK YOU GOD!!! ALL PRAISES TO YOU AND TO YOU ALONE!!!

Made in USA - Kendallville, IN
1079888_9781951941123
04.14.2020 1131